SACKCLOTH AND ASHES

THE BLOOMSBURY LENT BOOK 2014

SACKCLOTH AND ASHES

Penance and Penitence in a Self-centred World

ANN WIDDECOMBE

BLOOMSBURY

LONDON • NEW DELHI • NEW YORK • SYDNEY

First published in Great Britain 2013

A Continuum book

Bloomsbury Publishing Plc
50 Bedford Square
London WC1B 3DP

www.bloomsbury.com

Bloomsbury is a registered trademark of Bloomsbury Publishing Plc

Bloomsbury Publishing, London, New Delhi, New York and Sydney

A CIP record for this book is available from the British Library.

ISBN 9781408187166

10 9 8 7 6 5 4 3 2 1

Typeset by Fakenham Prepress Solutions, Fakenham, Norfolk NR21 8NN

Printed and bound in Great Britain by CPI Group (UK) Ltd, Croydon CR0 4YY

CONTENTS

INTRODUCTION

It's meant to be hard

The scene is a familiar one. Lent is looming and the same journalists who ring up public figures to enquire about New Year resolutions are now ringing to enquire about Lenten vows. I tell them I am giving up everything cxccpt water to drink. No alcohol, tea, coffee or fruit juices. Just fizzy Highland Spring.

The only unpredictable aspect of the next two questions is the order in which they will be presented: how much weight do I expect to lose and what will I do with the money saved? Each year I have to explain that it is not about weight or saving money: it is a penance. Drinking a glass of cold H_2O on a freezing cold February morning when all around you are gulping their cappuccinos and expressos is a penance.

'Oh, yes, that must be hard,' is the invariable response.

'Not as hard as Calvary.'

'Eh?'

I sigh. 'It's meant to be hard. It's *penance*.'

But what is penance other than the ritual of forfeiting chocolates in the run-up to Easter? What is its purpose? Is it an individual or collective activity? Is the quality of penance affected by whether it is voluntary or imposed? Does mortification of the flesh always involve the flesh? Can penance help towards salvation or is it only a demonstration of repentance or regret? Is there a difference between penance and punishment? Can penance enhance prayer? Is it a necessary precursor of forgiveness? Or is it simply a rather conceited, man-made distraction from an all-forgiving God, whose Son performed the penance to end all penance?

Today's world, at least in its developed areas, is about accumulating as much as possible as quickly as possible. The me-generation looks for rewards in money, celebrity and comfort. Credit cards take the waiting out of wanting. A whole variety of medicines and cosmetics promise instant relief, instant cure, instant youth. Patience is no longer a virtue highly prized but penance is impossible without it. For to be penitent involves a pause amidst the madness, time for reflection and for self-examination.

Our ancestors were comfortable with penance. In 1077 the Holy Roman Emperor, Henry IV, stood for three days bare-headed in the snow to persuade the Pope to reverse his excommunication. A century later King Henry II walked to Canterbury in sackcloth and ashes to be beaten by the monks as a penance for the death of Thomas A Beckett. Today our reaction would be to send for the men in white coats.

Eyebrows are raised at members of Opus Dei who still practise self–flagellation and I admit mine wander upwards too and I tut-tut about remnants of the Dark Ages but is penance really now no more than 40 days without a glass of wine or ten Hail Marys between confession and Coronation Street?

So what is penance in the twenty-first century? This slight volume, which is not a theological guide so much as a curious layman's exploration, seeks some answers.

I
PENANCE? ME?

In order to remember when Britain was not what has come to be called a Me, Me, Me society one probably has to go back to the 1950s and much maligned 1960s.

In the post-war years it would have been pointless to set store by material goods because they were in short supply. Everyone was in a permanent state of going without something and shopping was a carefully considered activity. For six years all anyone had been focussed on was surviving, on hoping husbands, brothers and sons would return, that both Hitler's bombs and the dreaded telegram would pass on by and once that was all over people craved only security and a gradual return to normality.

Not much was wasted. Sheets were patched, socks were darned and so were stockings and jerseys. School uniform was bought much too big and then worn until it was much too small. The washing machine boom had yet to happen and cleaning was sufficiently expensive for children to be told to make their clothes last a term during which time spills were sponged off. Taking everything off at the end of the day and dropping it all in the wash basket was unheard of. Clothes were handed down not only between siblings but between friends.

Central heating was not the norm and I can remember running between rooms to escape cold halls and landings and jumping over the floor to reach the warmth of the carpet (which was not fitted).

If material goods were not plentiful instant solutions were also few and far between. There were no credit cards to eliminate the tedium of saving up, no instant supply of antibiotics to kill infections, no faxes or emails to hasten the post, no mobile telephones to say whatever you wanted to say there and then, no self-correcting typewriters let alone computers. People were content to rent rather than immediately buy their houses, older children stayed at home until they married, families with a car thought themselves doing well. Britons holidayed at the seaside in Britain.

People with problems had no choice but to work

through them. Divorce was difficult to obtain and the process was messy, abortion was illegal, money hard to borrow. Families looked after their own especially their elderly.

It was all we knew and therefore we accepted it. With emails not even a twinkle in anybody's eye, we had to wait patiently for the post and for the operator to connect a trunk call and it did not seem at all odd. There were two TV channels not 200. Children played endless games of make-believe.

The adults had been through so much that there was a hugely strong sense of community and we looked after our neighbours as a matter of course.

I would absolutely not like to return to live in the 1950s but I sometimes find myself yearning for the days when we were not all in such a tearing hurry and not surrounded by the roar of unrestrained consumerism.

The 1960s brought hope and fun. Suddenly there was much more colour about – bright orange dresses and stiletto heels before, half way through that wild decade, dresses, handbags and bedlinen exploded into the kaleidoscope of colours dubbed 'psychedelic'. The shops sported an ever-expanding range of make-up, hemlines shot upwards, there was money to spare for pop records, tights replaced stockings and were discarded when laddered, carpets covered rooms, washing machines replaced red-elbowed women.

Prosperity was certainly arriving but so was something else – a rebellion against traditional morality, the beginnings of the *I can do what I want and it is nobody else's business* approach of moral relativism. Yet it was still an innocent decade. The Pill was in its infancy, drugs distrusted, abortion and homosexuality made legal only in 1967 and 1968 and divorce made easier only in 1969. There was wild talk of free love and trial marriages but the conventional order of marriage, setting up home and saving for children was still largely observed as was the woman's role in the nurture of children and man's as breadwinner. It was all much less daring than the picture many, usually nostalgically, paint.

It was the 1970s which saw the Me-culture take off as people decided to recognise nothing but their immediate need for 'happiness' which was often no more than a need for instant gratification or instant solution. Promiscuity became widespread. Why wait? So did the use of credit. Why wait? So did moving out of the family home at an early stage. Why wait?

The 1980s then added *I can have what I want* to *I can do what I want,* as Britain boomed, the enterprise culture blossomed and everyone believed he could be a millionaire by 30. The women were encouraged to be as competitive as the men and children were farmed out to childminders so Mum and Dad could both work.

Yet there was still the belief that in order to be successful you had to work for it. Fame, wealth and success were never going to be instant. Everyone envied the celebrities with their fast cars and faster lifestyles but very few dreamed of such success overnight. It was the era when managers, who used to consider it a symbol of their position to come to work at ten o'clock, began to come at six, a time hitherto associated with the workers. The Oxford graduate no longer considered it beneath him to set up a small business, even if it was window cleaning, because small businesses could become big, booming ones. There was optimism in abundance but based on an assumption that success followed the bright idea and the dedicated execution of it.

There was no national lottery producing instant multi–millionaires twice a week and no TV talent shows producing overnight mega-stars. Indeed Opportunity Knocks now seems almost village-hallish. If you asked teenagers what they wanted to be they might well have said something as ambitious and wishful as 'pop star' or 'model' or 'film star' but they would not have said merely 'celebrity'. There was still an assumption that fame and wealth followed success rather than being things in their own right.

At the beginning of the current century came *Big Brother*, the promoter of the culture of instant wealth and fame, then *Pop Idol*. Unknown, unremarkable, poorly-educated people could become celebrities overnight commanding millions of pounds and A-list status. I once joined poor Jade Goody for a TV programme and she asked me innocently not arrogantly if I was nervous at meeting an A-list celebrity! The result of such instant celebrity was that too many now aspire to it.

While all this was going on church attendance was steadily falling as people rejected the hereafter for the here and now. Between 1971 and 2007 the share of the population going to Sunday service fell by 52 per cent.[1] Religious education in schools also began to change, moving away from scripture to comparative religion as society grew both more secular and more diverse in faith. Indeed but for the requirements of law it is likely that religious education with a specifically Christian content and the daily act of worship in schools might have disappeared altogether. Atheism did not grow aggressive until comparatively recently but God was already being quietly sidelined.

The Lord's Prayer and the Ten Commandments were once considered basic literacy but when I recently made a documentary on Moses and the Law I found that many people struggled to name as many as two commandments. Hilariously when I did a *vox pop* around the Inns of Court only one lawyer remembered *Thou shalt not bear false witness against thy neighbour*!

---

1 See WhyChurch.org.uk

Now, in the second decade of the twenty-first century, there is not merely a culture of Me but a culture also of excess, which can be seen in any city centre on a Friday night when young women, scantily clad even in winter, fall drunkenly off pavements. I once did a radio programme in which I talked to young professional women who were utterly open about their weekly bingeing. Would they not feel a bit more dignified if they just had a few drinks? Say three or four rather than fourteen or fifteen? They looked at me as if I were speaking Greek. Dignity? Restraint? Was I straight out of Jane Austen?

There is no chance that any of them would offer up a penance of sobriety, for they saw nothing of which to repent! Rather it was I who spent the next ten days completely tee-total in revulsion at what I had witnessed.

So people want to have it all and plenty of whatever they like and, if challenged, will respond that it is a matter of choice even unto 40 or 50 handbags and pairs of shoes.

Fasting? Oh, yes, that is certainly still about but it is called de-toxing and has more to do with dress size than spiritual nourishment. Good works? Yes, people run marathons, for which they spend a long time training, in order to support a charity but the shortage of volunteers for the less dramatic kind of work is a constant headache for many organisations. Almsgiving? Yes, show me a tsunami and I will show you a tidal wave of generosity, but too often it is a pound in a collection tin on the way to buy a Mulberry handbag.

Church leaders have certainly been exercised upon the subject. The Roman Catholic Cardinal Cormac Murphy O'Connor actually suggested in 2009 that the recession might be a good thing if it caused a re-think and paved the way for a return of moral values, citing the then financial crisis as exposing the extent to which people are obsessed by money. He went on to say that in times of difficulty people had to depend on friends, neighbours and families and might thus re-discover what really matters.

Memorably he added 'if your worth comes from your wealth, that is not healthy. Your worth should depend on who you are.' He observed that shopping 'filled a void'.

He was not alone. The Archbishop of York, John Sentamu, blamed people for worshipping at 'the temple of money' while the Bishop of London, Richard Chartres, said that being made jobless in a recession can sometimes pave the way for leaving the rat-race.

Is it however just money? Are there other forms of selfishness that are creating the Me Society? What is the role of the explosion of social media? Facebook, Twitter and blogging have created an obsession with self as the centre of the day. Each move and thought is tweeted as if it is of importance and might be interesting to everybody else. People ignore others while they finish reading the latest text, spend social occasions glued to their tablets and walk along the street immersed in tapping and reading, oblivious of what is going on around them.

'You are less interesting than this' is the subtext of such behaviour on the part of people who would never dream of opening an envelope and reading a letter while sharing a meal with a friend.

Then there is the expectation of immediate attention. Those who send emails can be affronted if the other person is not sitting there and available to reply immediately.

'You took three weeks to reply' raged someone who had emailed me at the House of Commons. Indeed, yes, I did, because he was not a constituent, did not have a problem and had merely sent me his views. He was therefore at the end of the queue behind constituents' emails, letters, telephone calls and face-to-face meetings and also behind non-constituents with problems who had to be redirected to their own MPs and any letters I was writing or receiving on constituents' behalves.

Had he written conventionally, I doubt if the delay would have bothered him but the email society is an arrogant one.

Thus is Britain now: full of yearning for instant fame and wealth, chasing instant gratification, surrendering to excess, bombarding the world with news of one's own minute doings, expecting instant attention, unwilling to work out slow, difficult solutions.

I doubt very much if the average 15-year-old haunting the rails of Primark has a clue how to darn and a stockpot is less likely to feature in an average suburban kitchen than a Kenwood with all add-ons. Nor do soap jars adorn many bathroom windowsills. We throw away so readily that supermarkets have to bribe us to re-use the bags but they themselves fill bins with wasted food which has passed the sell-by date and which would be seized upon eagerly by the poor if only the poor were allowed to seize or the sick of the Third World to dose itself with our unwanted but perfectly serviceable medicine. Health and Safety dictates waste to a generation whose grandparents scrimped and saved.

Along with the desire to have it all *now* has grown also the desire to dispense with other forms of restraint. Girls have children by different men as if the babies were designer goods or meal tickets within the benefit system and the men proceed to give other girls babies without considering either the effects of growing up without a dad about the place or the probability of being able to support them. Relationships are dispensed with at the first sign of trouble and marriage is an optional extra. Abortion is available for 'social' reasons up to the twenty-fourth week. The State should look after

Granny, shouldn't it? After all, I've got my own life, haven't I?

Over the last 50 years first neighbourhoods disappeared, then the extended family living together and now even the nuclear family, within which it is regarded as a scandal – which the State should solve – if older children are still living at home. It is as if even living with other people with the necessary give and take involved is too much effort in twenty-first century Britain, where everyone wants to live in some individual paradise of one's own making!

The Early Church of course was dealing with a different kind of world and so is the missionary work which takes place in the Third World today. Often the reason advanced for the success of the African churches is the highly patronising one that the population has a simplicity of belief but that in a hundred years or so it will be as sceptical as Dawkins. What nobody seems to pause to consider is the effect of simplicity of living.

When life expectancy is low, daily living a struggle for existence and ambition limited to obtaining what is essential rather than desirable, the mind

17

tends to look for some meaning to existence that will make sense of it all rather than to the next shopping expedition. Retail therapy is unlikely to occupy those who have no clean water supply and who do not expect all their children to be alive if they themselves reach old age.

The profound irony of our times is that those without are more likely to do penance than those with plenty. The reason is that so many who have so much see no reason to inflict want on themselves, no matter how limited it may be.

'Why should I? What good will it do?' is the typical response to any suggestion of voluntary self-deprivation, a response based on greater respect for the body than the soul, on self-will rather on an outward–looking attitude.

One might be tempted to conclude from this that there is precious little penance around these days but if we scratch the surface a more hopeful picture can sometimes be found beneath the hurry and the self-centredness. In coming chapters I shall be looking at various definitions of penance but there are certain characteristics which have to be present namely: repentance, acknowledgement or confession of fault, and a desire to put matters right which might be termed either reparation or atonement. A fourth characteristic is amendment of life manifested by a resolution not to err again.

Let us be mindful of the gap.

When I was leaving school it was expected that we would go straight on to whatever the next stage was: university, perhaps, or teacher training college or nursing. Those who did go to university sometimes did Voluntary Service Overseas (VSO) afterwards but more often than not by then one was anxious to start work and the opportunity seemed to have passed. Now an increasing number of students and young people take a gap year, using much of it for volunteering at home or abroad.

It is not fanciful to imagine that the extent of the interest in volunteering, however much the prospect of travel and accommodation may play a role, indicates a strong consciousness of the needs of others, a desire to employ time usefully, and to acknowledge one's own multiple blessings compared to those who have so little. How much easier it would be in this age of student debt to spend the year instead in gainful employment.

I doubt if those thus engaged would describe such activity as penance but many might say that this is their last opportunity to do something useful before jumping on the treadmill of modern living, earning and spending. In a way, therefore, this is an atonement for the preoccupied life which will lie ahead.

Indeed penance is not much in evidence today as a conscious act, designed as such. Preoccupation with the self is the very basis now of our consumer-driven philosophy in which thrift is seen more as an interesting experiment or a harsh reality than a virtue, but what one might term subconscious penance is possibly more widespread than at first we might believe, if we are willing to define penance as a belief that humanity is selfish and that much could be done for the poor if only if it were less so and therefore one does one's bit to atone, even at the cost of some effort and inconvenience.

This involves subconscious confession: 'I am part of the great selfishness'; repentance: 'I should not be thus' or 'the human race should not be thus'; and reparation: 'I must do something about it'. Unless however there is some vague recognition that this is not what God expects the universe to be then it is purely secular penance, but penance nonetheless.

Such penance can take the form of good works – 'I must help others'– or of periods of self-restraint as in 'I have too much. I really do not need any more, even if I can afford it.'

Economists debate what is called in text books 'the paradox of thrift'. If there is a recession, people are more likely to save or at least to rein in their spending which means shops and businesses lose profits, which in turn means their workers lose their jobs, which in turn adds to the recession. It is, argue the daring, better to keep spending if you care about keeping people in jobs. Is there then such a thing as the paradox of penance? Might it be penitential to buy more food, more clothes, more goods, more fuel, more entertainment? Humph.

Most of us do it without even thinking about it. We 'support' our favourite small businesses in times of recession, not only as a mark of gratitude but because we want them still to be there when the recession ends. In short we help others for selfish reasons as well as unselfish, doing good in the hope that good will come out of it for ourselves, but as will be presently examined even spiritual penance can have a selfish edge; we want to turn away wrath and avoid judgement, to make it more likely we will make it into His kingdom, but that does not negate the act of contrition.

Then there is that other great advocate of restraint and inconvenience in the name of doing what is right: the environmental lobby, whose forecast of global disaster and a dire reckoning to come would outdo even Jeremiah at his most doom-laden. We are urged to repent what mankind has done to the environment and to amend our lives through acts of self-denial, such as buying only environmentally friendly goods, recycling into half a dozen different bins instead of cheerfully discarding into one, blocking up our wonderful real fires, choosing eco-lightbulbs, cycling instead of driving, even giving up air travel!

The most avid are doubtless driven by crusading zeal but also by an awareness of mankind's betrayal of trust by not taking care of the world we will pass on to future generations. Here we are talking less about atonement than a new way of life, one of the foremost aims of penance.

Indeed the State itself can do penance, inasmuch as it can repent and offer reparation. Sometimes this is quite voluntary but it can also be imposed. German war reparations are a good example of this, or when a court decides that the State has unlawfully imprisoned someone and awards compensation. By contrast an apology for slavery by countries which practised it to countries from which the victims came is likely to be voluntary.

It is also likely to be meaningless. Slavery has been acknowledged to be wrong since the middle of the nineteenth century and we are now in the twenty-first. The perpetrators and the victims are long since dead as are their immediate families. Where does it stop? Should we apologise to the descendants of those hanged for stealing sheep? Or to those whose ancestors were boiled in oil?

What would be the point of, say, the Russian leaders in 150 years' time apologising to the descendants of Sakharov or Solzenitzyn?

Should the modern Italian State apologise to us for the depredations of Julius Caesar or to all Christendom for the role of Pontius Pilate in handing over Christ to be cruficied?

So let us consider immediacy and stay with the society in which we now find ourselves, which, as I have already suggested, is not yet a complete stranger to the concept of penance.

Manifestations of secular penance such as the gap year spent in volunteering and the care of the planet would be unlikely to be recognised as such. Most people still associate the word with deliberate self-denial in the name of spiritual development and amidst the rush of the materialistic world which most of us in the West inhabit that is still familiar to the public only in Ramadan or Lent.

Ramadan, however, is not designed to be primarily pentitential, but rather the self-denial is supposed to remind the Muslim of his dependence on God. Lent, by contrast, is the last manifestation of regular, voluntary, spiritual, organised, mass penance in the modern world. So what does penance mean now?

2

From Canossa To Chocolates

We no longer trudge barefoot in the snow. These days we give up chocolates in Lent and consider that a challenge. But why do any penance at all? Let us look at the reasons commonly advanced.

God is Infinite Goodness against which the smallest sin offends. It is, Christ tells us, sufficient to call our brother a fool to be in danger of hellfire. Certainly Cain committed a significant sin when he slew Abel but if he had instead merely expressed resentment or anger then he would not have been sinless and nor is the man who, while eschewing adultery, indulges in lustful thoughts. The prospect of hellfire is not appealing so we must appease an angry God.

That is one view of the purpose of penance. Another is that we grieve His son every time we err, however fractionally, away from the straight and narrow and so we must give Him some tangible demonstration of our shame and sorrow; that somehow saying sorry is not enough; that after all He suffered on Calvary to save us from sin, we must show rather than just voice our love. We can't send round flowers so we must do something He can see.

Of course there is a view that penance is simply unnecessary regardless of whether we are worried about the penalties for sin (imperfect contrition) or devastated by having grieved the One who died for us (perfect contrition). Precisely because He did die for us, our sins are wiped away from the moment that we repent. It was a full, perfect and *sufficient* sacrifice. No suffering of our own can add to it. So better not to suffer then? Apparently not, because so many people who hold this view honour Lent.

They probably do so because penance can be an outward sign of an inner grace, that it enhances holiness and brings us closer to God as we voluntarily embrace a tiny share of His own suffering, that it directs our concentration on Him every time we engage in a penitential act. As fasting is believed to enhance prayer so penance enhances repentance.

Those then are the main claims for penance: that it turns away wrath, is a sign of shame and sorrow and enhances repentance and closeness to God.

It is perhaps important that we also consider what it is not. Penance is not a substitute for reparation where reparation is possible, it is not a bargaining chip to minimise wrongdoing, and it does not of itself without true contrition expiate sin (say ten Hail Marys and it's all over).

In her book, *Farewell to the East End*, Jennifer Worth of *Call the Midwife* fame, gives a moving description of a group of nuns in Germany after the war who were so horrified by what had been done to the Jews that they vowed to live as had the victims of the concentration camps, labouring intensively all day and subsisting on near–starvation rations. Were they trying to expiate the crimes of a nation? To turn away the wrath of God? Indeed can one's own penance atone for another's sin? Or were they simply so appalled by the magnitude of the offence against Infinite Goodness that they felt compelled to show remorse on behalf of the human race? Sadly I could not find anything further about them in my researches but I think that example of penance might be worth a book in its own right.

In the beginning was the Word and the Word is full of references to penance of which the most frequently recurring example, after sacrifice, is that of sackcloth and ashes.

Sackcloth was what nowadays we would refer to as a hair shirt: a horribly scratchy material made from goat hair. Indeed, for centuries after those we shall presently consider, holy men wore a garment made out of hair as a penance to 'mortify the flesh'.

The Old Testament Book of Kings shows us Ahab rending his clothes in horror and clothing himself in sackcloth when Elijah prophesies his doom because he has aroused God's anger by killing Naboth and seizing his vineyard. (1 Kgs 21.27) The purpose and the result was the turning away of God's wrath and the remission of the punishment as foretold by Elijah. A similar purpose motivated King David and the Elders when Israel had sinned and they donned sackcloth (1 Chron. 21.16) but there is another theme here for the same clothing was used also to symbolise mourning in the Old Testament so they were also mourning their sins.

The book of Nehemiah offers us an example of collective penance when the people of Israel assembled in sackcloth, fasting and with earth on their heads, repenting not only for their sins but for those of their fathers, (Neh. 9.1) while in Jonah not only the king and his subjects but even the animals of Ninevah were covered in sackcloth when the prophet told them they had just 40 days left before utter destruction. (Jon. 3.7 and 8). It proved a good move because God relented.

So it would appear from the descriptions of penance in the Bible that it can be an individual or collective act but there is in none of the above examples any suggestion that a third party can do penance for the relief of another's individual sin. David and the Elders were representatives of the sinning Israel, not substitutes, so the more modern example cited by Jennifer Worth works only because the nuns in question were themselves German. A group of English nuns living in the same fashion in penance for the wickedness of the human race in general would

29

be acting symbolically rather than representing the wrongdoers directly.

Furthermore the nuns were offering penance as a collective act for collective sin, not to expiate the individual sins of, say, Goering or Goebbels.

The distinction is important when looking at the history of the mediaeval Church with its profoundly corrupt practice of the sale of indulgences. The theory was that X could deprive himself of his money and thereby remit a portion of Y's punishment in purgatory.

In the Philippines in 2011, the Catholic Church proclaimed a national day of penance to atone for an exhibit in an art exhibition which was deemed blasphemous. The Church was not responsible for the exhibit so again we are looking here at another act comparable to the Elders repenting for the sins of Israel and the nuns for the sins of the holocaust.

But the New Testament is consistent in its teaching that we face judgement individually, or as the Catholic Church describes it 'a retribution in one's own soul'. Christ's suffering redeems us but only upon condition of individual repentance. We will return to this theme later when examining what, if anything, a sinner can add to that full, perfect and sufficient sacrifice.

Although there is a great deal about punishment, penance, as a voluntary rather than imposed act, could be said to be sparsely treated by the New Testament, being largely confined to Christ's chiding of Chorazin and Bethsaida (Mt. 11.21) but that is true only if one is looking at penance as a self-imposed suffering or deprivation. There is however a great deal about fasting, an act of self-denial which, as practised by Christ himself, is the foundation of our modern Lent.

It is clear from the writings of the early Christian church that penance was very much part of the approach to sin and Tertullian, writing in the second and third centuries AD, is still talking of sackcloth and ashes.[1] A century after that Eusebius recounts an incident of a penitent in sackcloth and ashes.[2] The theme therefore of some outward sign of repentance is consistent.

---

1 Tertullian *De Poenitentia* Ch.9.
2 Eusebius *Historia Ecclesiastica.*

If we further broaden the definition to include doing what we do not want to do in the name of loving our neighbour then the examples in Christ's teaching are plentiful: going the extra mile (Mt. 5.41), giving away the second coat (Lk. 3, v.11), turning the other cheek (Mt. 5.39), leaving the gift at the altar while making good a quarrel (Mt. 5.23 and 24).

Are these acts of charity only or also penances? If we do not want the second coat then clearly there is no penance involved but if we cherish it then we deliberately deprive ourselves. Why? Only because we are sorry for the man with no coat? Or because we recognise that it is greedy to keep two and repent of our ways? Or perhaps we hope God will notice and chalk it up on the right side of the ledger? Or is it an act of thanksgiving, a demonstration of gratitude that we can afford the second coat?

Penance can indicate that a person is conscious of sin or of sinfulness. The two are very different. By and large we do not observe Lent in reparation for any individual sin. One does not say 'I am giving up alcohol for Lent because I lost my temper with Auntie Mary.' One gives up pleasures or takes on burdens in Lent as a recognition of general sinfulness and of the looming commemoration of Calvary which redeemed it. The same is true of fish on Fridays. Catholics do not abstain from meat on Fridays because they have committed a specific sin but rather in recognition of general sinfulness and of its consequence on that Friday more than 2,000 years ago.

That sort of general penance causes us no embarrassment. We do it quite publicly, but I have yet to hear anybody say that he or she is abstaining or fasting to demonstrate repentance for an act of, say, adultery. Yet looking back at the two historical examples I have touched upon, Canossa and Henry II's punishment, the penance was for a very specific sin.

There has therefore been a significant change in our thinking, whereby individual voluntary penance for individual sin has become a private act. Public acts are reserved for penance of the imposed variety and these days are imposed by State as punishment rather than Church as part of a sacrament. A collective public act as demonstrated by the Philippines example above is still acceptable but if today somebody were to make a bare-footed pilgrimage to say, Lourdes, for any purpose other than raising money for the church roof it would be little understood and respected only warily.

Where would the post-1963 life of John Profumo fit into this picture? Having become entangled with vice-girls, lied to the House of Commons and effectively brought down a government, this ex-minister spent the rest of his life working at and for Toynbee Hall in the East end of London, combatting poverty. This was a public act in as much as everyone knew he was doing it but he was left to get on with it largely in private. Its significance lies in the respect which he so comprehensively won as a result. I remember being on Any Questions when the announcement came through of his death in March 2006. My tribute to him was applauded by all sections of the audience.

Profumo could have let the dust settle and then sought a career elsewhere, being eminently qualified to do so, but chose instead to devote himself to good works. It is difficult to see this as other than penance and the public approbation as other than an acknowledgement of full expiation.

Twelve years after the scandal, Profumo was awarded the CBE in recognition of his charity work. Twenty years after that he was seated next to the Queen at Mrs Thatcher's seventieth birthday party, the general consensus being that he had not only fully redeemed himself but that his life had been both good and useful. Whether today he would have been allowed to make amends in such a fashion is doubtful when an intrusive and gloating press follows a fallen man's every move, inviting comment from all and sundry.

Many a less publicly recognised act of similar penance has taken people of all ages to the Third World. Sometimes the motivation is simply to help the most vulnerable in all the globe but often one hears sentiments expressed which suggest also an element of penance. Some aid workers have spoken of how offensive they find western affluence when they return home. They are not merely helping the weak but also distancing themselves from the strong, seeking to justify their own abundant blessings by voluntarily giving them up. If one were to suggest to such people that they were performing penance on behalf of the selfish world they would probably deny it.

Yet even if unrecognised, penance is lurking there beneath the layers of motivation.

Public penances imposed by the Church were discarded by the first Lateran Council in 1123 but the requirement for private penance has survived in varying forms across Christendom. One will not see much sackcloth and ashes about the place but in both religious and secular life there is an enduring belief that penance is an answer to sin.

3
I Want To Do It

Penance as an individual act may be either voluntary or involuntary, a demonstration of repentance or an offering of chance suffering on another's behalf. One of the joys of Catholicism is the concept of 'offering it up'. Such suffering may be trivial but the cause may be great.

'Offer it up for Indonesia,' urged Sister Mary Evangelista when I fell over and cut myself at Bath Convent. I remembered the exhortation well enough but not the context, so when writing this I looked it up and found that 500,000 people had died in that country as a result of political unrest. Somehow I do not think my cut knee would have been of any great comfort to the relatives.

While however we may offer suffering to alleviate another's, there is, as already observed, no suggestion that one individual may expiate the sin of another specific individual through penance. Performing penance as a recognition of the sins of mankind in general as well as one's own against Infinite Goodness is to demonstrate a general sense of unworthiness but bargaining with God on behalf of another's soul is found largely in discredited practices such as the sale of indulgences.

Penance involves several stages and this chapter will look purely at voluntary penance, that act which an individual chooses to perform of his own free will.

The first stage is repentance. Put simply, one really is sorry that one has said, thought or done something sinful. A secular approach would be to say that one is full of self-disgust at having fallen below one's own standards but this is not what moves the Christian penitent. Self is not the issue or at least not the primary issue: the sin is detestable because it offends or grieves God, because it necessitated Calvary, because it is a fall from grace and not because it offends merely oneself or lowers an individual in his own self-assessment. Such sentiments may be present, but they will be incidental.

Without true sorrow penance is meaningless.

Jokes abound in the Catholic Church about confessing the same sin week after week, carrying out the imposed penance and believing that is the end of the matter but that is to make a mockery of penance in any real meaning of the word.

The next stage must be to put right what one has done where this is possible: to restore a reputation destroyed by slander, to pay back stolen money, to apologise for loss of temper, to take back a lie, to break off an adulterous relationship etc. Penance without reparation where the latter is possible throws doubt on the first requirement – repentance.

If there is no desire to right a wrong then how sorry can one be for it?

So, if A steals from B and knows where B lives then he cannot keep the stolen items and expiate the sin by a day's fasting. That seems straightforward enough but let us now reverse the situation. Supposing he returns all the stolen goods, is that itself a penance? Does the act of reparation remove the need for any further demonstration of regret? If there cannot be penance without reparation can there be reparation without penance? Or does reparation always by definition contain an act of penance?

This is possibly best addressed by considering various scenarios.

1 John steals money from Mary. He then repents and returns it secretly so that she has no idea who took it.
2 John has spent all the money before he repents. He has no means of earning its replacement so he sells a treasured possession and from the proceeds returns Mary's money.
3 John takes the money, cannot replace it and has nothing to sell so he goes to Mary and confesses what he has done, offering to garden and decorate until the debt is paid.

The first of these possible responses to awareness of sin is an act of reparation but involves no penance. John suffers neither loss of face nor property. He gets away with reparation at no cost to himself, Mary gets her money back and everybody is happy and relieved as the status quo is restored. So what could be the purpose of penance?

In any sin there are at least three parties involved: the sinner, the victim and God. So far in this story God has been sidelined. There is no doubt that if John seeks His forgiveness, then as truly repentant, he will receive it but we are here looking at voluntary penance so John may decide that he will give the equivalent of his theft to charity or to deprive himself of something he enjoys for a specified time. His salvation cannot be said to depend on it but he is trying to show God that he is sorry, as did David and the Elders when they donned sackcloth and ashes.

It is worth a pause at this point to consider just how rare is that practice of penance, certainly for everyday sin. The reason is not hard to discern: our lives are so full of impatience, covetousness, anger, envy, selfishness, hurtfulness, disobedience, lies, deceits, to name but a few common transgressions that penance for each instance would mean a perpetual state of mortification, which is likely to be embraced only by living saints or monastic orders. So we lump our petty sins together and get rid of them by a single act of contrition in private prayer, the sacrament of reconciliation (when one confesses to a priest) or general confession. In our story John is only

41

likely to volunteer an act of penance if he deems the sin big enough, as this one is. Yet Christ told us that just feeling angry with someone can imperil a soul!

In the second scenario, John has performed a penance in order to effect reparation by selling that which he does not want to sell. Had he regarded the item with indifference then no penance would be involved. Interestingly, this option would be unlikely to be inflicted by either Church or State. A priest would not insist on the action in return for absolution and the State might make a compensation order but John would not have to satisfy it immediately. He could pay Mary back over time, thus prolonging her loss. Even if Mary sued and sent in the bailiffs, John could already have moved his treasures to a place of safety. So in this scenario, John, through an act of voluntary penance, is causing himself a pain which nobody else would.

It is worth noting that this type of penance may occur through either secular or religious motivation.

Much the same can be said of the third situation above, but here John is doing penance in the open, not publicly but certainly with Mary's knowledge. He has added an extra dimension of mortification, one which our ancestors insisted upon: visible shame. The Church has long since abandoned such a requirement but the State has not, as we shall see when we look at imposed penance. One again three parties are involved: criminal, victim and State. Neither religious nor criminal law acknowledges transgressions as being solely between perpetrator and victim.

Today penance is a relatively light-hearted business. We resent giving up our favourite things for Lent, have daily wrestles with temptation and can occasionally feel deprived and cross, but we also enjoy it as a challenge, counting off the days, feeling pleased when we succeed, revelling in any likely health benefits. Catholics will discharge the prescribed number of prayers and then dash back to the daily routine. Nothing is much interrupted. Our normal preoccupations continue. The above example works only because both secular and religious persons recognise the sin as significant and therefore worth a pause.

Whether or not an action can be classed as a penance is determined by its motivation. Let us consider the man or woman who decides to sleep rough for a night or to live on benefit levels for a week. It could so easily be a penitential action but very rarely is. The usual motivation is to 'show solidarity' with the poor or homeless or to 'draw attention' to their plight in the hope that somebody else, namely the government, will help them. I know of no case where the cardboard-box-sleeping celebrity has said to the chap in the next box, 'Come home with me and sleep in my spare bedroom, until we can sort you out.'

I do, however, know of a Christian MP, Ken Hargreaves, who used to invite vagrants to share his home and was rarely let down by theft or anti-social behaviour. He did so just because he felt he should, but it was not a penance.

However, someone could sleep in a shop doorway all night as a penance for the selfishness of the human race which lets people drift off society's compass or for his or her own selfishness in being focussed on material wellbeing. The uncomfortable challenge then becomes to mend one's ways but at least the man or woman in this example has paused and considered the offence to Infinite Goodness, even if the next step is a

Full English breakfast, followed by a hot shower and clean clothes.

Motivation then is key but it brings us back to that first requirement of penance: repentance. The man who sleeps rough to try and shame the government is effectively saying that he has no personal shame in the matter, that he feels sorry for others but without any consciousness of personal sin or of being part of a collective sin. Repentance in one's own soul is the precursor of voluntary penance.

After repentance and reparation comes resolution: a commitment not to offend again. Penance without that commitment is again meaningless for a sin cannot be expiated if it is not also detested. The success of the resolution is less material than the strength of the desire to avoid a repetition or as it is called in the Catholic Act of Contrition 'to avoid the occasions of sin'.

In this example John gets drunk and acts aggressively, frightening people. As a voluntary act of penance he gives up drink for a week, then resumes his old habits, gets drunk, becomes aggressive and frightens people. He is sorry

45

enough to offer penance but not enough to try something a bit more radical. In modern parlance he hates himself afterwards but just can't help it.

In this example the chances are that even as he reaches for his pint, John is praying for forgiveness but he still drains it and asks for another. The notion of praying 'May God forgive me' as one embarks upon sin is an interesting one for it suggests either simultaneous sin and repentance which is understandable, or that one sins deliberately and hopes for forgiveness in advance which is less so. In this category would certainly fall the supposed penitent who believes that it is all right because at the next confession he will receive absolution.

In probably the most famous example of all time, Pontius Pilate tried absolving himself in advance by washing his hands as a symbol that he divorced himself from the atrocious injustice which was to come and in which he was about to play a pretty decisive part.

I admit to feeling sorry for the chap who certainly epitomises the peril of being in the wrong place at the wrong time. But for that posting to Jerusalem he would have been just an obscure Roman governor, his name known only to scholars of the period. Instead, 2,000 years after he handed in his scroll to Tiberius, his name is uttered by millions across the globe every Sunday in a less than flattering context.

Nevertheless he stood poised between doing what was just or unjust and took a political decision in favour of the latter. The hand washing must stand for all eternity as a symbol not of disengagement but of hypocrisy. Hypocrisy, however, despite the pronouncements of the tabloid press, is not the sin against the Holy Ghost.

If Catholics talk about the occasions of sin, Anglicans ask for time for 'the amendment of life'. In secular parlance people 'sort themselves out' or 'get it together'. Whichever term one employs the objective is the same: to leave undesirable conduct behind. In the secular world there is supposedly an answer for everything: the gluttonous take up diets, drunks go into rehab, the unfaithful move jobs or locations, the lazy find a personal trainer, the spendthrift locks away her credit cards, the office bully trails off to a people awareness course. And, as anyone can tell

47

you, if the resolution is not truly present none of it helps in anything other than the short term.

We are not called to be successful but only to be faithful, to paraphrase the late Mother Teresa. A resolution can fail but one seriously and earnestly attempted is the third stage of penance.

So there we have the three 'r's: repentance, reparation, resolution. The result of penance is the fourth 'r' – redemption. Perhaps then this is the moment to look at the greatest penance and redemption of them all. Calvary.

4

THE PENANCE TO END
ALL PENANCE

For 40 days, Christ hungered and fasted in the desert. That would not have been penance as we have been discussing it for He was without sin but was rather an enhancement of prayer as he began to prepare for His ministry, a ministry that would culminate in His taking all the world's sins on his own self and, by dying horribly, atone for them to His Father, thereby paving the way for mortals to have eternal life.

That, pronounces one branch of Christian thought, is enough. The sacrifice of the cross is full, perfect and *sufficient*. The price of our sin has already been paid and so acts of penance are superfluous if we hope by them to atone for our sins. They may be fine as a demonstration of shame and sorrow but they contribute nothing towards our salvation for that has already been comprehensively secured. We can no longer turn away God's wrath by whatever we now substitute for sackcloth and ashes. Whatever our sins, there is no practical part played by penance in their remission.

That is a rather simplistic explanation of the doctrine of justification by faith, which I shall presently look at in greater detail. If we believe in Him then our sins are remitted from that moment. Needless to say the same approach utterly denies the existence of purgatory and any suggestion of penance after death. In short this mode of thought says being sorry is always enough.

Christ's suffering was manifold: physical torture from the crown of thorns to the agony of a Roman crucifixion, humiliation from mockery and jeers, temptation from those who urged Him to prove Himself by coming down from the cross, and the unspeakable mental torture of watching His mother and faithful friends in turn watching and grieving for Him, knowing that they did not understand. There can be no form of human suffering which He did not endure in the passion. Not only did he take on Himself all sin but all suffering too.

It is worth pausing at this point to reflect on the agony of Calvary and especially one that is often all but overlooked: that of knowing you are letting down those you love, that you could do otherwise but that duty demands you choose instead to see the disappointment and bewilderment in their eyes. It is important because there may be applications for us in considering some aspects of penance such as reparation.

One of the sharpest pains we can endure is that of watching others suffering on our behalf. The man dying in agony of incurable disease will be as distressed by the mental and emotional sufferings of his family as he is by his own physical ones. However unavoidable the disease may have been he will feel, irrationally, that he has somehow let them down, that by succumbing to the illness he has deserted them and has left them with unbearable memories as well as an uncertain future.

How much sharper does that pain become when the suffering is caused not by misfortune but by deliberate act. The bewilderment in his children's eyes and the misery in his wife's will haunt many an occupant of her majesty's prisons long after he has forgotten what the foreman of the jury looked like.

If either the man on the sickbed or the felon in the dock could miraculously take away the sufferings his condition were causing his nearest and dearest then can there be any doubt that he would immediately do so?

When we think of Calvary, we think first and foremost of the hideous suffering of a Roman crucifixion, of a slow death lasting for hours without even a millisecond's relief from pain. Perhaps also we think of the humiliation, of the degrading dragging of the cross through the streets, the jeering crowds, the mocking soldiers, the gloating Sanhedrin. We marvel at the courage of the victim who forgave the perpetrators, who endured the agony without complaint.

And His mother watched it all, noticing every twitch of agony, hearing every unuttered groan, each stab of His pain an arrow through her own heart. And as she watched Him so He watched her watching Him, understanding the sheer grief which consumed her, knowing that she did not share His knowledge of the coming resurrection, that she did not understand why He was dying in so unspeakable a fashion. He could miraculously have taken that pain away. He could have come down from the cross. Yet He did not. He let her suffer on because He knew that what He was doing addressed a greater wrong, served a greater cause, that eventually she too would rejoice in that terrible death.

Mary would not have been the only sobbing, confused sufferer on that first Good Friday. There were also the Apostles, then merely disciples. For three years they had followed a man whom the crowds adored and the authorities feared. Only a few days earlier the people had hailed Him and strewn palm leaves in His path, cheering Him to the echo. Now those same people had howled for His death and the quaking authorities had won.

It must have baffled them, Peter, Andrew, James, John and all the others. Above all they must have felt so very badly let down. This was the man Who had performed all those miracles, had walked on water, Who had even raised the dead. Yet now He seemed helpless.

Some of them might have had very different expectations. They might have thought of Him as the one who was going to rid their land of the Roman invader, as a future king, as the long awaited

Messiah who would, of course, deliver Israel in a manner which they understood, who would free his people from Caesar as Moses had freed them from Pharaoh – but without the awful inconvenience of wandering in the desert for 40 years.

Others may have had less specific but equally happy expectations.

To be with Jesus was to be always with the winner, with a man Who caused crowds to sit spell-bound for hours as He preached, Who could cure any ill, Who so satisfyingly routed the Pharisees in debate. Now He had let them all down, was leaving them to go back to whatever it was they had been doing before He called them. The glory, the hope, the expectation, the devotion were over. Some may well have been angry as well as gloomy.

Some speculate that Judas may well have betrayed Him in order to force His hand, confident that by that treachery he was bringing forward the hour of Jesus's triumph. So shattered was he by the very different outcome that he took his own life.

Jesus could have put an end to all that anxiety

too, could have come down from the cross, confounded Pilate and all the Roman officials, defeated the machinating Jewish authorities, restored the crowd's faith in Him and the disciples could have returned to His side in the centre of all the adulation. Yet He did not. He knew what was expected of Him, knew what was right and knew the two things were quite different.

Then there were the ordinary people. Those who had called for Barrabas to be released instead of Jesus might be ruing their action. Those who had bravely called for Jesus would have been feeling let down. This man, they would be thinking, was not after all the Messiah, just another rash fool who had upset those with the power to crush him. So where did that leave them? With no hope, no solace, no expectation of some wonderful event with which to leaven the grind of their daily lives. Some would have shrugged, some wept, some sworn, some would pity the forlorn figure on the cross and others would curse Him for fooling them, then letting them down. All would have felt forsaken.

He could have put an end to that at once but He did not. In a just cause the pleas and curses of the crowds, even the oppressed crowds, must come second to what was right.

One of the great lessons of Good Friday is that we must be prepared to let people down, to disappoint those whom we love, to refuse to live up to the expectations of others if by doing so we do what is right.

Of course Christ Himself had been let down. His best friends ran away at the moment He was being seized. He was betrayed by, of all things, the kiss of a follower. He listened while the man closest of all to Him swore by all that was sacred that he did not know Him. That, however, was different because so much of it was involuntary. His friends ran for cover because they were scared. Peter may have been a lying coward but he had at least crept along to see what was happening rather than desert his master altogether. Jesus knew they behaved from weakness only but His own behaviour was that of full intent. He knew what He was doing, had the power to act differently but resolutely held to His course.

It is a test that confronts most of us in minor ways all our lives: the decision to follow the right course rather than the one others may expect, to stand out against the wishes of family, friends, workmates, political party, to be an irritant rather than to conform. For others it appears in a vastly more dramatic form and can shape history.

'For goodness sake, do what the king asks and come home,' begged the wife of St Thomas More, unable to understand the principle which drove him to prefer the Tower of London and a traitor's death.

'For goodness sake, Winston, let it alone. People don't want another damn war.' Thus was the sentiment with which Churchill would so often have been confronted when standing out against appeasement in a country, which was still recovering from the devastating effects of a conflict which had ended but 20 years before.

'Wilberforce, you're just not getting anywhere. Give it a rest.' I wonder how many said that as time after time, year after year, anti-slavery measures were ground to dust beneath the chariot wheels of the economically motivated and the careless tread of public indifference. It was an opinion which would have been uttered not in irritation alone but out of concern, out of friendship, out of feeling for Wilberforce. And he looked his friends in the eye and said no.

'Yes, of course it's awful what they are doing to Jews but, darling, you mustn't get involved. Do you want to put the children at risk? Do you want the SS coming for *them*?'

We should each ask ourselves what answer we would give to that last question. Surely the ultimate in letting down is not merely to desert but actively to put at risk those we love.

Yet the legacy of Calvary was just that. After His ascension, Christ left behind a collection of followers and their families who were never again to feel safe. Indeed the very friend who swore so volubly that he did not know Him was to be crucified upside down after many years of defying the authorities in the name of Christianity.

For most of us the tests are, mercifully, not so harsh or demanding, yet looking those we love in the eye and deliberately disappointing them when we have a choice to do otherwise is still one of the most difficult things we have to do.

The child of a traditional Asian family in which she has been loved and nurtured and decides she does not want an arranged marriage faces a pressure much greater than any her family can bring to bear – that of letting down, hurting and disappointing those she loves. She looks into her mother's tortured eyes as Christ looked into the eyes of Mary as she wept by the cross.

The medical student proud with academic honours tells his father he is not, after all, going to become a world famous heart specialist but prefers to take his gifts to a third world country and heal in obscurity. He is and always will be grateful for all his family have done to ensure his success – the financial sacrifice, the emotional stability, the encouragement, the general being there – but he cannot live as they had hoped.

The politician who takes a stand on an issue which is so contrary to his party's that it must deny him the successful career on which his friends and followers had relied; the whistle-blower who calls down opprobrium on the very people she works with day after day; the parents who finally betray a criminal child to the police; the single one in the new group of trainees who will not agree to the inflated expenses claim; the child with the strength not to follow friends into something forbidden; and so many others in so many situations disappoint, hurt and bewilder family or friends or just those who rely on them.

It is easy to underestimate how great a hurdle this must have been for those who have brought some of the biggest and best changes to the history of the human race; easy, for example, to sentimentalise Florence Nightingale as the lady with the lamp and to forget that to take a group of women to a war zone to nurse the wounded men of both sides was a defiance of social norms and expectations so gross as to cause them initially to be shunned and reviled. Similarly, Elizabeth Fry defied every last convention to bring succour to prisoners.

If any of these people had settled not only for a quiet life but had preferred the happiness of family and the good opinion of friends over their own notions of what it was right to do then we would all be the poorer. Without the willingness of Jesus Christ to let others suffer the most extreme misery for His sake there would have been no salvation, no hope of eternal rest, no reconciliation of God and man.

Therefore during Lent as we prepare both for the sacrifice of Calvary and for the celebration of the resurrection by enduring some trifling penance of our own we should perhaps look beyond the nails, the scourge, the crown of thorns, the thirst, the muscles aching with the unbearable pain of the weight of the body, the jeering and the mockery and instead think of what then appeared as the greatest let-down of all time and of its utterly deliberate nature. Then we might reflect that it was carried out not by an angry young revolutionary but by a man who was all compassion, all caring, who understood suffering and who identified with the poor and oppressed.

Let us think of Mary watching Him and of Him watching her watching Him and know that this was by no means the least part of that great sacrifice: that one of the most important examples He left us was to look those we love in the eyes and, in the full knowledge of the hurt we cause, to let them down.

Penance can often involve letting others down: confession and reparation may mean causing those who once had high opinions of us acute disappointment. Any resulting humiliation from the intervention of the justice system can cause the penitent to see a fraction of what Christ saw in His mother's agonised eyes in those of his loved ones.

Yet Christ's terrible penance on our behalf, in all its physical, mental and emotional anguish, does not end penance but rather makes salvation available to the penitent. Repentance, reparation, resolution and, where appropriate, penance are still the expected responses to sin. The early Church required and exacted penance. Over time our concept of proportionality has changed but the essential principle has not. A Catholic priest will not withhold absolution until a penance is complete but he will expect it to be carried out as an outward sign of repentance, as a recognition of sin.

I am classing such penitential acts under the heading of voluntary penance because the sinner goes willingly to the priest and therefore is indicating willingness to perform penance. Such acts might be prayer, an offering, works of mercy, service of neighbour and voluntary self-denial.

It may seem odd to count prayer as a penance but the intention is that the sinner keeps an awareness of his sin in mind when praying, that he focuses on growing in spirituality in order to effect amendment of life.

The aftermath of penance is a new life, one in which the sin is no longer a burden. The aftermath of Calvary was the resurrection itself, the dawn of hope of eternal life.

The concept of redemption through suffering is by no means confined to Christian thought. Rather it is a recurring theme of literature and drama throughout the ages. Take, for example, Somerset Maugham's *The Painted Veil*, in which a shallow socialite betrays her husband, who then forces her to accompany him into a cholera area. Unwilling and selfishly preoccupied at first, Kitty undergoes a personal transformation as she is exposed to the example of selfless nursing and sacrifice.

Who could forget Sydney Carton redeeming a wasted life with that ultimate act of self-sacrifice in *A Tale of Two Cities*? Or the fate of the Ancient Mariner? Wherever we look we find redemption purchased through self-sacrifice or suffering. Is this simply a hangover from history, in a country where the Church once reigned supreme, or is it a basic human instinct to believe that the route to redemption is through a repudiation of the past and best exemplified by acts not words?

Yet if the concept is abundant in literature, penance appears to be the Cinderella of artistic inspiration when it comes to painting. It is not a theme often found, in contrast to the Last Judgement (when it is of course a bit late for penance!) which was prolifically covered in mediaeval and renaissance art. Michelangelo, Lochner, Memling and van Eyck were just a few of the many artists who turned to the Second Coming and final disposal of souls for inspiration but in Christian art there is little by way of the depiction of penance.

La Penitente by an unknown artist shows a young girl with clasped hands and downcast eyes, but it has hardly the message of Hatsuhana praying under the waterfall (discomfort enhancing prayer) or the penance of Hercules (effort to expiate wrongdoing). It would seem that if we want to look at penance through art then we must travel beyond the realms of Christianity!

A glance across the religious map confirms that the concept of forgiveness through repentance and the embracing of a new way of life is not confined to Christianity. The Christian is born again and from that moment his past sins are wiped out. The convert to Islam, that sternest of religions, is absolved of all previous sin at the point at which he becomes a Muslim. In Hinduism and Buddhism the concept of sin itself is much less clear cut but interestingly the idea of penance through discipline and spiritual torment is strong. The one common thread is a consciousness that wrong doing offends God, the source of all goodness.

Yet from the earliest times it is clear that the Christian way of life involves suffering as a means of amending life. The young man who came to Christ and told him that he had observed the commandments from his youth up but knew he still lacked something was told to sell all his possessions and follow Him. It was insufficient merely to be conscious of a need to do more: Christ required a serious degree of sacrifice, which in this case was a penance too far for the sinner.

That story, which is found in the Gospels of both Matthew and Mark, is too often seen as being merely about love of material possessions but it is about vastly more than that. Christ did not say to him live more simply or share your goods with the poor or up your almsgiving: He demanded of the young man that he give up all that he had, that the sacrifice must be total.

Elsewhere Christ tells us it is a blessing to be reviled and persecuted for His sake and urges those who would follow Him to 'take up their cross' a symbol of suffering. The new life, it would seem, involves a great deal more than repentance alone. Calvary bought mankind's salvation but that is just the beginning not the end for mankind's duty to confront and overcome sin.

The early Christians could hardly have been in much doubt about what might be required: St Peter was crucified, St Paul beheaded, St Stephen stoned while their followers cowered in catacombs. From the earliest saints to St Thomas More to the long procession of those burnt at the stake to Bonhoeffer under Hitler and to Wurmbrand under communism to Christians in Pakistan today, the thread of preparedness to suffer and if necessary die has been a continuous one.

And we give up KitKat for Lent.

Yet all of that without Calvary would have been meaningless. Mankind alone can never atone for sin, nor offer any sacrifice to wipe out its wickedness. Only sinlessness itself could do that and Christ was without sin. Offering penance is not to diminish Calvary but to try and share in a tiny part of it.

So can being sorry alone ever be enough? At first sight Christ's parable of the prodigal son suggests that it can be. Off went the chap in question to spend his inheritance in riotous living and when he has blown the lot and finds himself with barely the shirt on his back he recognises the follies of his ways and decides to go home and say sorry, whereupon he is feted by his father with a fatted calf.

A second glance however suggests a rather different interpretation. The son came home in full expectation of serving a penance of being employed by his father as a hired servant, of living in his father's house but without recognition as his son, of seeing his brother treated as family while he must be at his beck and call. Such penance was remitted but the sinner was willing to embrace it, willing to expiate sin. In our example in the previous chapter Mary could have told John she needed no reparation but the willingness to put right a wrong would still have been present, a readiness for penance.

We have looked at repentance, reparation and resolution but as this parable shows there is a fourth element involved: confession. The prodigal son greeted his father with the words 'I have sinned against heaven and against thee and am no longer worthy to be called thy son.'

Laying aside the collective confession found in Christian liturgy and guilty pleas in the criminal justice system, the overwhelming majority of confession these days is a private matter. It may occur between sinner and priest or between sinner and God alone but it has not always been so. The writings of St Augustine are full of confessions about everything from apple scrumping to sexual misdemeanours. The baring of the soul in material designed for public consumption went out of fashion for centuries but is now back, in a highly secular form, in the outpourings of celebrities describing addictions, marital infidelity and raw emotion leading to bad or even criminal behaviour. Indeed some women's magazines would be empty if shorn of such content. So, one suspects, would TV programmes such as the Jeremy Kyle show.

Often the tone is not remotely repentant and the aim neither to expiate nor to seek forgiveness. Rather, the motivation can often be expressed in pounds and pence or in satisfaction derived from revenge. Even where those last are not present there is very rarely any plea for pardon but rather for understanding. Shoplifting, betrayal, lying and cheating are all paraded as deserving of sympathy.

Confession as a precursor of penance is motivated by a desire for forgiveness, an awareness of wrongdoing, a sense of something alienating one from God. The Catholic sacrament is described as reconciliation, a restoring of closeness between Deity and sinner, a re-admission to the presence of Infinite Goodness and the plea is not for sympathy but for mercy.

Repentance and confession are important concepts for understanding the relation of human penance to that offered on our behalf on Calvary. Human penance in isolation from repentance and confession can have no validity. It must be preceded by a genuine sorrow, a claiming of that terrible but full, perfect and sufficient sacrifice. Penance is a demonstration of repentance and cannot be a substitute for it.

That much was taught clearly by the Early Church but somewhere along the line and quite quickly repentance and confession began in themselves to be terrible punishments. Christ said to the woman taken in adultery 'Go and sin no more' after freely forgiving her. To the thief next to Him on Calvary he said 'this day shalt thou be with Me in Paradise.' But in the first centuries of the Church's existence the love and mercy were replaced by rituals which emphasised the sinner's position as outcast.

In AD 96 Clement of Rome wrote to the Corinthians and exhorted them to 'Be subject in obedience to the priests and receive discipline unto penance, bending the knees of your hearts.'

A hundred years later it was not just the knees of the heart which were being bent. Tertullian is by then talking not only of sackcloth and ashes but of prostrating and humiliating oneself, of fasting and weeping for 'whole days and nights'. Indeed, by now in the Eastern Church penance was a progress, with sinners divided into four groups.

First there were the flentes (weepers) who remained outside the church begging the faithful to pray for them. Next came the audientes (listeners) who had progressed as far as being allowed to the back of the church to hear some of the Mass but not to participate in its most solemn rite of communion. The substrati (prostrate) received the laying on of the bishops' hands while the consistentes stayed throughout but did not take communion. Crumbs! Whatever happened to *judge not lest ye be judged*?

In the West these unhappy divisions were not recognised but banishment from communion was normal, in deference to St Paul's terrible warning that to eat and drink unworthily was to eat and drink to one's own damnation (1 Cor. 11.29).

Today excommunication is rare and serious although Catholics are urged to abstain from communion if they carry the burden of an unabsolved grave (or mortal) sin and the divorced can still be banned. Any weeping or prostrating would almost certainly be met with whispers of 'hush' or uneasy shuffling in seats.

By the fifth century matters had reached a pitch where even the dying were being put through a series of hoops before being absolved, a situation which scandalised both St Leo and St Celestine and indeed seemed to be at odds with the decrees of the Council of Nicaea.[1]

Ten centuries later it was normal for absolution to follow immediately upon confession and penance had ceased to be a necessary precursor to forgiveness. It was beginning to assume its modern form.

---

1 The Council of Nicaea was the first council of all Christian Bishops summoned by the first Roman Emperor to become a Christian, Constantine I, in AD 325. Among its decrees is Canon 13 which states that anyone nearing death shall not be deprived of communion.

With the reformation came a sharp divergence of views on penance in relation to Calvary and one's ability to contribute to one's own salvation has remained part of the debate on what is known as justification by faith. Theological arguments have this much in common with political arguments: they turn fine distinctions into deep divisions and this is certainly a prime example.

This being a book designed for the general reader rather than as a contribution to theological thought, I am going to simplify the complex and resist the temptation to explore each and every nuance of this centuries-old dispute.

Justification by Faith is, essentially, the teaching that by believing in Christ's sacrifice your sins are at that point forgiven and you are saved. Nothing else is necessary, no good works, no penance, no actions. You are born again and assured of heaven.

Christ Himself however made it clear that to enter His kingdom it was necessary to do the 'will of His Father' (Mt. 7.21). He also pointed out 'by their fruits ye shall know them' (Mt. 7.16). St James spells it out very clearly when he writes

'What good is it, my brothers and sisters, if a man has faith but no works? Can such faith save him?' (Jas 2.14).

So good works are necessary but that to me is a statement of the blooming obvious, Gov. It is quite impossible to imagine anybody whose faith is real making his life a no-go area for good works. The dispute only becomes interesting if one turns the question round and asks if anybody can be justified by good works alone, i.e. without faith.

Christ gave us a pretty big hint when He said that whatever we do unto the least of men we do unto Him. We have already looked, in another context, at the rich young man who would not give up all his possessions to follow Christ. Not all his belief could save him. Works were required. We will be judged not only on what we believe but on how we live our lives.

At this point the reader may be tempted to respond that this is all very interesting but what has it to do with penance? Look no further than Profumo whose penance was a lifetime of good works.

Indeed in Lent, the Church's penitential season, the Church does not ask us only to give up something but also to increase our almsgiving and do good. So there is a rather different dispute which does not much engage church leaders and theologians but tends to be central to most people's Lenten resolutions: is it better to give up or to do something positive? Is visiting the sick or helping out at the Hospice really classifiable as penance? Indeed should good works ever be viewed as a penance?

Perhaps if we clean the homeless centre once a week we can keep on munching the chocolates and swigging the wine? This however is a discussion which I shall postpone for it is germane not only to voluntary penance but to the involuntary variety too.

For now we must look at the State penitentiaries, as they are called in America, a major characteristic of which is that a large number of people in them are not remotely penitent.

5

PENANCE AND THE LAW

*P**oena* is the Latin for punishment, compensation and expiation depending on its context. However much the nature of punishment has changed over the millennia, its aims have stayed fairly constant: retribution, deterrence and redemption.

Unlikely as it may seem, for much of our history redemption was even believed to be encompassed in capital punishment. Christ said that those who received approbation on this earth had already had their reward and those who were rich had already received their comfort and faced woe in the next world. Thus grew a widespread theory that punishment on this earth could mitigate punishment in the next but there is no evidence that this, rather than retribution and deterrence, was the driving factor.

As was observed in the third chapter both Church and State consider a third party to be involved in any commission of crime, in the former case the offence is against God and in the second against the State or society. A person who has completed a punishment imposed by a court of law is said to have 'paid his debt to society'. The law takes retribution out of the hands of the victims and administers it on behalf of humanity as a whole.

Retribution does not negate forgiveness and it is possible to be both punished and forgiven but the underlying principle of retribution is that crimes must always produce consequences, which is another way of saying that penance must always be exacted.

Hitherto we have been looking at a situation where penance is a sign of sorrow and repentance, of a consciousness of wrongdoing, but now we are looking at the enforcement of penance on those whose only sorrow may lie in the fact of being caught and in being obliged to undergo penance. In such cases it is an act wholly divorced from repentance and is a sign not of an individual's displeasure with himself but of the State's displeasure. Even where a criminal is indeed sorry for the deed rather than the detection, and even if the victim seeks no revenge, the State will consider it must still act on behalf of itself.

One of the reasons for that is deterrence: the example made of the transgressor to deter him from any repetition of the misbehaviour and to deter others who may be thinking about committing the same crime. The second consideration is of paramount importance in the case for capital punishment.

Although some still argue that a life for a life is a sound basis for the death penalty most are convinced that human justice being fallible its punishments should not be irreversible. However the deterrence argument introduces a different moral dimension. If it can be shown that the existence of a capital penalty is of a sufficiently deterrent nature to save lives then the choice lies between saving innocent life and saving that of the guilty.

Arguments about the death penalty apart, however, deterrence remains entrenched in criminal justice systems. Is it a notion confined only to imposed penance or has it a role also in the voluntary manifestation? When an individual does penance for a specific sin is he seeking to deter himself from repeating it? Were the poor old flentes of the early Eastern Church serving as an awful warning to others with their all too public exclusion?

The answer to both questions is almost certainly yes, that the principal difference between imposed and voluntary penance is not the existence of deterrence but its overt acknowledgement.

Redemption and expiation are incorporated into imposed penances in two ways. The first is in the concept of a debt expired: one is not punished for the same crime twice. A punishment completed equals a crime atoned for and the wrongdoer is almost as free of it in the eyes of the State as is the believer at Calvary in the eyes of the Church. Almost but not quite, for the crime against the State remains on record and the crime against Infinite Goodness does not, a theme to which I will be returning. The second, however, is of more interest in modern penal systems: amendment of life, or as it is more generally known these days, rehabilitation.

This noble aim may be found emblazoned on the gates of every prison in this country. '....To help them to lead law-abiding and useful lives in custody and after release'. It is the second part of the mission statement of Her Majesty's Prison Service, the first being about keeping prisoners securely where they are supposed to be.

The divergence between theory and practice is depressing as attested by the dreadful recidivism rates of some 47 per cent for those leaving custody re-offending within two years – and that statistic is limited to proven re-offending. Amendment of life does not appear to be a normal product of imposed penances involving custody and the figures for non-custodial sentences are no more reassuring. Why not?

What is going wrong?

The Church teaches that the sinner must look at the causes of sin and try to avoid them. The State is supposed to provide a similar analysis with prisoners gaining insight in to their crimes and 'addressing their offending behaviour' but limited resources and teeming jails make it all a bit difficult.

There is a number of offending behaviour courses including anger management. Additionally there are special group sessions for sex offenders and some programmes to combat drug addiction but the majority of prisoners will either have no access to such courses, be moved around before completing them, or be released with no equivalent facility in the outside world. This is particularly deleterious for young offenders who tend to return immediately to the very environment and peer group which caused the problem at the outset.

Purposeful activity is nearly always the first casualty of an overcrowded prison system whereby staff have to give priority to security and prisoner movement rather than to daily occupation and amendment of life.

The voluntary penitent has already made an assessment of his own wrongdoing but the prisoner can pass through the entire penance without concluding such analysis worthwhile, while others who have assessed his needs can be thwarted by the pressures of the system from addressing them.

The Devil finds work for idle hands was a favourite maxim of my grandmother and the truth of it may be seen daily in the criminal justice system where the idleness often begins well before the crime. Up to 75 per cent of those who come into Her Majesty's prisons are either illiterate and innumerate or, if not quite that, are wholly without qualifications and the most basic levels of education.

They have truanted away or been excluded from – and usually a mixture of the two – vast tranches of their secondary education and generally all the latter part of it. The alarm clock has played no part in their lives and the concept of an orderly, structured demanding day is alien to them. Often, but by no means always, they come from an environment in which that is the norm for the neighbourhood, where they have been taught by example to believe that aspiration is either not available to them or is a mug's game when it is possible to 'live on the social'.

This way of life is not a source of regret to those living it but they have not been helped to consider the alternatives, which they vaguely believe to be the preserve of the rich or clever, and they are failed catastrophically by the State.

If they truant they will be lucky to be caught and compelled to return. The enforcement of school attendance in this country is a hit and miss business, depending largely on the resources and priority accorded to it in whatever area the truant lives. Many parents connive but it is often the helpless who are fined rather than those who contribute deliberately to the problem. If the pupils are excluded it is all too frequently the case that there is no immediate education available to them. The more fortunate will find a place in a Pupil Referral Unit, the unlucky will be left to idle with an unfulfilled promise of a few hours' tuition a week.

So what do the truants and excluded do? They will get up late, seek out friends in the same situation and hang around the streets. In those circumstances drugs are never very far away and with the drugs comes the need to pay for them and the next stage is the shoplifting at which point they are on the conveyor belt of crime, from which they may not fall off until it is too late.

To lock such people up in idleness and then expect them to mend their lives is cloud cuckoo land. Every prisons minister and Home Secretary knows it but there are no votes in prisons either literally or metaphorically. It is a short-sighted attitude for, as I said in my Party Conference Speech when I was Shadow Home Secretary, rehabilitation is not and has never been some soft, wet, liberal optional extra. Rather it is a crucial tool of public protection for if the man who comes out of prison is as likely – or possibly even more likely – to commit crime as the one who entered the gates then the result is more crime, which in turn means more victims and more expense for the taxpayer as future sentences are funded.

As with offending behaviour courses, so with prison work and education. In some prisons it will be plentifully supplied and in others only very sketchily so. The chance to glimpse a different way of life, based on structure and the acquiring of skills, is for too many simply not there.

In the world of Widdecombe every convicted prisoner would have to do a full day's work every weekday either in the prison education department or in the workshops or, preferably, in some combination of the two. The work that came into prison would be real work supplied by real contractors for delivery to real customers as a result of which we could pay real wages and from them take real deductions. That would then enable prisoners to learn not only the routine of a working day but also the orderly distribution of earnings. As it is all we do is exact penance without offering the opportunity of redemption.

In this the modern penal system, however much kinder, differs little from that devised by our forebears, who believed that the punishment itself would supply the will to change. The harshness of the regimes and the cruelty of the physical punishments have, by the grace of God, gone but the purpose has not much changed: custody protects society by keeping the miscreant out of action and may or may not deter him from such action in the future but focussed attention on the causes and occasions of sin is not much more in evidence now than it was when Elizabeth Fry walked the earth.

Not all penance exacted by the state, however, is designed around custody: cautions, fines, suspended sentences and community work all play an increasing role.

'Go and sin no more', is the implied exhortation behind cautions. There is no punishment, just the drawing of the sinner's attention to his transgression with the warning that next time he may not be so lucky.

A suspended sentence is also a manifestation of 'go and sin no more' but this time with judgement attached, an assessment, so to speak, of the sin's severity. Here punishment is not remitted but rather held in abeyance for a prescribed period of time during which the wrongdoer must show he has amended his life and is capable of resisting temptation or forfeit his liberty.

The Old Testament is, as we have seen, replete with examples of sinners either individually or collectively averting a punishment which God had pronounced He was going to deliver by using the time between rebuke and enactment of the sentence to demonstrate repentance and to turn away the wrath of God. With a suspended sentence the state is offering that same chance. The criminal can turn away the wrath of the state.

Most fines are the secular equivalent of a couple of Hail Marys or the adult version of a tap on the wrist from an exasperated but not yet angry parent. They are rarely punitive and are the means of inflicting inconvenience on the individual rather than the state, which will thereby not have to supervise a community sentence or find a custodial place. If they are genuinely unpayable they will not be paid. In short they are, by and large, the lightest penance the state can impose.

Community work is largely centred on reparation or, in modern parlance, on payback. The sinner must put something back into the society he has offended and that, rather than direct reparation to the victim, is the philosophy behind the sentence in the majority of cases. He is not yet an outcast and can live normally with his family, going to work and maintaining his wordly goods but he must give up his time to make life better for others.

There is more than just reparation involved. He may not be cast out like the flentes but he is humiliated as were the substrati, for the penance is public and the hairshirt a high-visibility jacket. The self-righteous can sniff in disgust at prisoners but a 15-foot wall will muffle the sound and the sight. Those on community service are less lucky: many must operate in the full glare of the public to whom they are offering reparation.

Others will not and will be allocated work in care homes where those assisted may not distinguish between them and the normal staff. In their case the penance is not just the quiet payback but an opportunity to consider the plight of those less fortunate. In some cases this exposure to suffering leads the wrongdoer to continue the work long after the penalty has expired.

Thus it is also with voluntary penance. The person who decides to 'do good' rather than 'give up' for Lent may find the habit lasts well beyond the ringing of the bells on Easter Sunday and that what began as a time-limited penance brings a lifetime's habit of willing service to others.

Interestingly the person who discovers a new interest through community work may still err again and still keep up the interest. The proven recidivism rate is at the time of writing some 35 per cent and has been known to be on a par with that of those released from custody and to rise to over 50 per cent.

With no punishment offering much more than mixed success there has been a growing demand for new thinking and that thinking has been centred around the relationship between the wrongdoer and the wronged.

In this chapter we have been looking at the state dealing with crimes committed against society but what about the individual victim? Sin is against Infinite Goodness and crimes are against society but what about the casualty in either case? There is much talk of victim-centred justice but not much in the system that is directly relevant to it, other than the satisfaction of seeing a miscreant punished.

Look at the causes of sin says the priest, address your offending behaviour says the Home Secretary, but what about the consequences of wrongdoing? The impact on others? Both Church and State encourage the sinner to examine his own soul, his own behaviour, and his own moral worth, but should a greater emphasis be given to the one on the receiving end of crime?

Feelings of jealousy, rage and hatred are always sins but not crimes unless acted upon. In the first case the victim may be unaware of being a victim but a crime more often than not leaves someone feeling at best ill-used and at worst frightened, deprived and upset.

I pass over victim compensation orders as being, even when fully implemented, tokens rather than instruments of reconciliation. The more challenging idea is that of restorative justice.

6
LOVING OUR NEIGHBOUR

Christ's teaching was that we must love our neighbours as ourselves and that if we hold anything against another human being we should seek reconciliation with him and if we cannot resolve the disagreement we can then seek the intervention of those in authority. We must deal mercifully with others (the parable of the two debtors in Mt. 18.23–35) if we are to obtain mercy for ourselves.

He spoke also about judgement and about being held to account for lives at the end of them and at the end of time.

The combination of these commandments appears to suggest that we should be aware of the impact of our deeds and to be prepared to make amends. Restorative justice places the focus of this back on the relationship between the individuals involved as perpetrator and victim in crime. It can occur in custody and as part of a sentence in the community between a criminal and his own direct victim or between a group of criminals and a victim of similar crime.

It can occur not only in the criminal justice system but in schools, as a diversionary tactic as much as a punitive tactic and as a tool for social services as much as for probation officers. It is found in violent crime and in petty crime, in youth offending and in dealing with long-term recidivists but, despite all that, the application of the principles may be wide but the practice is not as widespread as some would like it to be.

If thou has aught against thy brother, go and tell him his fault. Thus did Christ prescribe the process of reconciliation but that works only if you know who is responsible for the deed, if you know who your brother actually is.

The woman who lives alone and returns from work to find her house ransacked and small treasures taken will suffer a large number of immediate emotions: anger, disbelief, misery and fear. What has happened once can happen again so it may be a very long time before she approaches her home in the evening without wondering what she will find, and a long time before she can look at her windowsill and not miss the precious vase that was her great grandmother's and which was smashed in the course of the thief's entry. She may miss her mother's engagement ring not for its financial value but for its symbol of the love between her parents which formed the background to her own upbringing or, worse, she may have recently suffered a bereavement and find the theft a violation of her memories of that dead husband or child.

In the midst of all this she is likely to ask the investigating police officer 'do these people *ever* think about what they do to us?' Restorative justice gives her the chance to put that question directly. She can explain either to the man who burgled her house or to a career burglar who has not been directly responsible for her own experience, how she feels and what the long-term impact is, and he will have to listen and respond.

The purpose of this is twofold. It is a process which obliges the wrongdoer to think about his crime from the victim's point of view and it offers a degree of healing to the victim. There is also a view that it is much more difficult to offend against an individual once one has been obliged to view him as a person rather than simply an anonymous being. The assumption is that having been obliged to face up to the human reality of the victim the offender will think twice about creating another victim in the future.

Large claims have been made for this practice in terms of its role in preventing re-offending, but it is a very lengthy and time-consuming process and because, as with other methods of treating crime, it can fail it is not regarded with universal enthusiasm.

Reparation in the delivery of justice is nothing new, as we have already seen. From Ancient Babylon to Ethelbert of Kent, our ancestors understood the principle of making good the damage caused by crime, of making restitution of property an integral part of punishment. King Hammurabi was the first to codify it (c. 1772 BC) with his decrees that a man who flooded his neighbour's crops must make good the damage and in the sixth century AD Ethelbert likewise decreed compensation for damaged property but today's restorative justice seeks a different sort of restitution: an emotional healing, an ability to consign both crime and consequences to the past.

The aim of restorative justice is that the perpetrator comes to empathise with the victim and as a consequence is deterred not by penalty but by moral insight from repeating the crime. Once he has got to that stage the aim is then that he and the victim should look into his original motivation and perceptions. This may assist not only the criminal to take control of his life but the victim to understand the man behind the crime.

These same principles can be applied in contexts beyond both victim and offender, especially but not exclusively when dealing with young offenders where there can be an impact on families. In the mid-1990s I watched a family conference which was taking place under the restorative justice system in which the various members were explaining to the miscreant in the presence of a trained mediator, why he could no longer live at home. It was a very long process and would have been quite impossible to replicate in each and every case.

Restorative justice is now global and can be found in Canada, Australia, The UK, Brazil, Uganda and Hawaii to name but a few countries, but its value appears to lie in individual healing rather than in any measurable impact on crime rates, enabling the victim to forgive and the offender to want that forgiveness. The concept satisfies the requirements of St Matthew's Gospel in as much as individuals address their differences and resentments rather than leaving it all to the impersonal ministrations of the state, but it makes little impact where society wants to see it: in overall crime reduction.

Restorative justice meets all the criteria of penance: confession is vital for clearly the process cannot begin at all unless the offender admits his crime. Repentance may not necessarily be there at the beginning of the process in any real sense of the word but as empathy with the victim grows it will follow. That will lead to the desire to make reparation in whatever ways may be possible and finally by obtaining forgiveness there is healing and reconciliation. That is why the church is an enthusiastic supporter but the State wants results in an overall reduction in the harm which crime inflicts on us all.

If resolution between victim and offender face to face can be effective can the same feelings of repentance and empathy ever be generated when the crime is victimless? Can the State or the Church be a collective victim with similar needs for restitution?

Go to enough dinner parties and there are some questions which are bound to arise sooner or later. Along with Have you ever seen a ghost? comes Which era in history would you like to visit and If you could commit a crime and know for certain that you were not going to be caught, what would it be?

Let us lay aside for a moment the belief that God sees all and therefore there will always be a reckoning. Lay aside too any practical considerations of feasibility. For these purposes we must discard both Deity and reality because the real question here is can you commit a crime which has no victim? And can you commit a crime, even knowing there would be victims, without feeling guilty, without any feeling of the need for penance?

The most common response to this is to say that one would raid the Bank of England, after hours when nobody was about to feel alarmed, help oneself to the contents of the vaults and then give it all to the Third World. Robin Hood lives on.

I would respond that I would destroy every single abortion clinic in the country, having first ascertained that nobody was inside any of them. The method of destruction would have to be very quiet and unalarming to the neighbourhood but as we are talking theory not practice that need not hinder the plot.

Another might say that he would steal all the animals in all the zoos and release them back to the wild.

The possibilities are numerous but what we have in the replies are examples of the conflict between conscience and obedience to the law. Put conscience first and the State will exact penance but one may not oneself be conscious of any sin, indeed one might well rejoice in what others see as wrongdoing. One has violated the law but in a cause one regards as greater and even where people suffer as a result (all the zookeepers would lose their jobs and their families would be deprived) the perpetrator believes the overall impact to justify that. In its extreme form this may be found in one man's freedom fighter being another man's terrorist.

Clearly if we all lived only by our own laws there would be anarchy so the State can be a victim but so can the Church, which like the State, will decide what is right and wrong but in so doing will not please everyone. It is possible for even the most obedient of believers to say 'I just do not believe that is a sin. I love my neighbour in the Third World too much to let him starve or I love the helpless unborn child too much to let it be killed or I love all God's creation and zoos are cruel.'

From which can only follow: 'therefore I do not repent. I see no sin to confess and I will do penance only for form's sake not from any conviction.' The secular equivalent is 'it's a bad law and I do not care if I go to prison.'

In these circumstances penance reflects neither healing nor absolution but merely punishment divorced from any resonance in heart and soul.

I can do no other. Luther's words as he pinned up the 95 theses and prepared to take on the entire religious establishment in an age when religious dissent could be cruelly punished reverberate down the centuries but the exasperated exclamation of his examiners paints the real dilemma: *surely a single monk must err if he stand against all Christendom?*

The penance in those days could have been burning at the stake but it was easier to defy that than the still, small voice of his own conscience.

It was not a victimless defiance. Christianity plunged into civil war from which horrors such as the Saint Bartholomew's Day massacre in Paris and the slaughter of the Anabaptists emerged. Even Catholics will recognise that the church was in dire and urgent need of reform but it is arguable that it was happening anyway, albeit slowly and that, defining the church as the body of Christians rather than merely the hierarchy, it was a victim on a grand scale. Did Luther forget in his eagerness to serve God that the same God had commanded him to love his neighbour or, in an age where life expectancy was low and life itself cheap but the soul reverenced as immortal, did he simply think it all a price worth paying?

Who is my neighbour? asked the man who inspired Christ to the parable of the Good Samaritan. The victim in restorative justice might well ask the same. Must he love and do good to the man who has robbed him? The aim, as noted, is that he will indeed learn to forgive the man who has wronged him through the healing process of the face-to-face discussions but supposing the victim is instead left in ignorance of who harmed him or sees his tormentor only across a courtroom. What is the role for forgiveness then?

The paradox of an age of moral relativism is that forgiveness is in short supply. *Pure evil, lock him up and throw away the key, I hope he rots in hell.* Such sentiments are now the standard fare of newspaper headlines. One of the casualties of the decline of biblical literacy is the diminution of the emphasis we place on forgiveness. Indeed when we encounter examples of it in difficult circumstances we marvel.

We are all familiar with the faces of some who have never forgiven. Ann West (the mother of Lesley Anne Downey who was abused and murdered by Brady and Hindley) or the mother of poor little Jamie Bulger are obvious examples), but all too frequently we encounter the phenomenon in the language of those whose sufferings are much less extreme. Forgiveness allows people to move on, to lighten their own lives and, in the case of those who cannot forgive on behalf of others, to live perhaps as those others would have wished.

Yet forgiveness of others is also part of the process of penance. *And forgive us our trespasses as we forgive those who trespass against us* is the clearest linking of our own absolution being dependent upon our remission of grudges against others. So is the parable of the two debtors in which a man is excused his debt and then demands the return of a lesser one from another, impervious to his pleas. Outraged, the first creditor delivers him to punishment. The lesson is clear enough: what was forgiven at Calvary is greater than anything we might ourselves be asked to forgive. The theme is continued in the admonition about motes and beams.[1]

---

1 *Motes and Beams. Gospel of St Matthew ch7 v.3. Sermon on the Mount. 'Why beholdest thou the mote that is in thy brother's eye but considerest not the beam that is in thine own eye?'*

To be forgiven we must also forgive. Without our own willingness to love our neighbour enough to forgive we cannot reach the final stage of penance which is reconciliation.

History provides some wonderful examples of forgiveness. St Paul gave the early Christians a pretty rough time but they embraced him upon conversion with which happy outcome we are all familiar. Had they decided not to do so then all those wonderful epistles would have been lost to us and Christianity would have taken much longer to reach the countries on his missionary trail.

Two thousand years later Pope John Paul II forgave the man who had tried to kill him as did Gandhi a rather more successful assassin. Corrie Ten Boom shook hands with a guard at her concentration camp while the daughter of Anthony Berry, a Conservative MP killed by the IRA during the Brighton bomb atrocity, made public reconciliation with his murderer, Patrick Magee, and they have now set up a charity *Building Bridges for Peace* which promotes reconciliation.

There is even a website devoted to worldwide forgiveness which records the case of a victim of a drunken driver receiving him in friendship even as he was lying in hospital with every bone broken and punctured lungs.

Some years ago I made a programme for BBC Radio 4 on the subject of forgiveness and interviewed a man who had forgiven his daughter's killer, but I also interviewed others who said no, it was impossible to forgive, particularly where the injured party was a loved one.

In the secular world people talk about letting go and moving on. The Church calls it letting go and finding peace. It is the last stage of penance.

So loving our neighbours is a prerequisite of the reconciliation which consummates penance but can it ever be the penance itself?

7

DOING GOOD: PLEASURE OR PENANCE?

The role of doing good in the criminal justice system, where it is regarded as 'payback', has already been examined, but its role in voluntary penance is rather more complex. We are commanded to love our neighbour so is looking out for his needs love or penance?

Those who prefer to 'do' rather than 'give up' for Lent may choose various courses of action: a Catholic might decide to go to Mass each day rather than once a week; people might give to charity over and above their normal amounts; they might pray more or set aside time for meditation; they might give time to help a charity or they might find time to help someone directly.

How much of this can be described as penance? As with giving up, positive action can be measured as penance in terms of its impact on one's life, either in the short or long term. Is it hard, inconvenient, mortifying? Or being none of these things does it enhance awareness of others to a point where it also enhances reconciliation or spiritual peace, in other words does it produce amendment of life? Does it demonstrate repentance?

Most people, whether believers or not, will have encountered challenges to their complacency in the face of suffering. We see advertisements for charities begging for funds in the intervals which punctuate our favourite TV programmes, but as the distressed faces and emaciated bodies fill our screens we are dashing to the kitchen to switch on the kettle, stir the supper, return a phone call. Then comes a big, one-off disaster and we are sufficiently arrested in our daily occasions to stand, stare at the unfolding scenes and then give.

Those who give to or work for charity in Lent are effectively forcing themselves to pause without the catalyst of disaster. To donate more to others means to spend less on oneself but it will be the extent to which this is the case that will determine whether or not it is sackcloth and ashes or whether it is money that will not be seriously missed.

Even if it is the latter it may still be penitential, an act of repentance for selfishness, an acknowledgement of sin, the equivalent of a passing but sincere 'sorry'.

To repent is to be aware of Infinite Goodness and extra time laid aside for prayer and meditation in Lent fulfils that. Even if the time is not much missed there is still a pause, a turning away from self.

Sacrificial giving, praying until one is too tired to pray longer and giving up all leisure time for the execution of good works will instantly be recognised as penitential because it feeds into our perception of voluntary penance as self-inflicted punishment, but as we have seen throughout this book, penance is about more than penalty.

All these acts, whether undertaken punitively or lightly embrace the essential elements of penance: confession, repentance, reparation, healing.

The driving motivation has to be a recognition of one's own selfishness which is another way of saying a person confesses it, for if one brushed it aside no action would follow. 'I am selfish and it is wrong' is the precursor to the rest. Similarly if one did not repent this lamentable trait of character then again no action would follow. The extra pound in the charity box or five minutes on one's knees is a demonstration of repentance and also of reparation. Of course it is better if it is not entirely token but even a token deed indicates awareness.

What happens next is known in the secular world as 'feeling better about oneself'. Christians call it healing, reconciliation, drawing closer to God, which is the last stage of penance.

Those who embrace direct action for Lent or in penance for a specific sin or as a result of a sudden shock in the face of suffering are similarly divided between those who fit in what is convenient and those who strain to encompass all they set out to do. The action itself is also divided between direct aid to individuals and aid to organisations which address a particular problem. So is it just the time and inconvenience which are penitential? How can voluntarily helping somebody possibly be a penance in its own right?

I once encountered a man who spent many an evening walking the streets of London where the homeless huddled in doorways, handing out food, the occasional gift of money and advice about shelters and sources of help. He told me that he was always pleased to help and that the odd success here and there, when a youngster returned home or someone used a shelter as a springboard to a new life, was all the reward anyone could want. Then he added a telling sentence.

'Sometimes, when a cold wind is blowing and the rain is drenching me and my fingers turn numb, I really feel exhilarated. They are the most satisfying times.'

Eh? Did he mean that was when the homeless needed him most? No, he meant that if he suffered in the course of his perambulations, then he thought he really had made an effort. He felt better about himself. What he had done must surely be more pleasing to God than if he were wandering about on a balmy night, even though in each case the objective – the relief of the poor – was exactly the same.

It is a neat demonstration of our attitude to loving our neighbour, that somehow we feel so much better if it isn't all plain sailing, if it is in some way *penitential,* or as I was taught at Bath Convent, if we can offer it up.

What I believed in this case was that whatever satisfaction he might have got from inclement weather and chilly fingers, this man was genuinely motivated by his concern for those less fortunate than himself. Supposing however he wasn't? Would that somehow have made his actions more worthy of the description of penance?

Most of us have some causes to which we are naturally drawn. They may be political or charitable but we are naturally and effortlessly outraged or moved to compassion. We may acknowledge other concerns but it is a blessing for the human race that we all focus on different ones and resent neither the time nor the money which they claim from us. We want to do it. We are called to do it. We would be amazed if somebody called it penance even if much sacrifice is involved.

Take the case of Lucy Fensom. Lucy was an air hostess with British Airways (BA) who noticed on visits to the Middle East how abominably the population treated donkeys. Unlike horses and camels they were not regarded as noble beasts but rather as mere goods and chattels, worked nearly to death and then discarded by the roadside. With no animal welfare laws and an absence of understanding even very basic needs in terms of food or treatment, the donkeys stood no chance.

Lucy would not have been the first Westerner to notice and to grieve but she was the first to act. Giving up her job with BA, she moved to Israel and formed a sanctuary which is now home to more than 100 donkeys. A team of vets goes out giving free check-ups and advice, while another group of volunteers visits schools and gives talks. The upheaval and risk which Lucy undertook, huge though such an undertaking was, in no way seemed merely a duty or a penance for the human race: Lucy acted solely out of love for God's lesser creation.

His greater creation has benefitted too. Once two Palestinian boys found a donkey dying by the wayside and remembered the sanctuary because their school had received a visit from one of Lucy's team. Unfortunately the beast could not move and they were at a loss how to get it there (this was before the Wall) so they approached an Israeli soldier who hefted it on his truck and transported it to the sanctuary where it recovered. It was a wonderful act of hope in a conflict-torn world.

However, now let us posit in the previous example that the man is not much bothered by the plight of the homeless, that he believes there are enough shelters and charities working on their behalf and that if they prefer not to take advantage of them that is their problem not his. He would prefer to give his time and alms to those who have no control over their misfortune: the disabled perhaps or those without wells in Africa.

Then one day his conscience is stirred. What right has he to judge those whose strategically-placed polystyrene cups implore his aid? He decides he may have been a bit too dismissive and forces himself to stop and talk to the chap huddled in the next doorway and from there his conviction grows that there is something he can do and, perhaps unwillingly at first, still disgusted by the empty bottles of booze and the rank smell of unwashed flesh and clothes and the lingering conviction that those on the streets have a choice about being there, he decides to make an effort on their behalf.

That is penance and when people talk about doing good for Lent they generally mean helping in an area outside their usual voluntary activity or perhaps increasing what they already do to a degree that would not be normally sustainable.

Now let us revisit our man and the homeless some years down the line. He is now spending most of his spare time in helping the homeless. He still gives to charities for the disabled and the African waterless but his passion is the homeless in UK cities. His original unwillingness is but a distant memory. He has thus moved from penance, as a conscious renouncing of his early attitude, to charity, motivated solely by love of his neighbour.

It is well-known that Barnardo was moved to set up his homes for children because a child he had turned from his door died. Undeniably this was an act of repentance as well as charity and it was a repentance which brought hope to thousands. Niemoller repented of the way he had stood by and watched as the Nazis came 'first for the communists, then for the Socialists and Trade Unionists and then for the Jews' and his writings are richer as a result.

'Of all the acts of man,' wrote Thomas Carlyle, 'Repentance is the most divine. The greatest of all faults is to be conscious of none.'

The very word penance is full of negative associations but, as in this example, it is a hopeful act which can be a source of happiness rather than just voluntary or imposed punishment. We see the same outcome in both the religious and secular worlds. Family members fall out with each other, bear grudges for years and then illness, bereavement or some other misfortune compels them, however unwilling they may be, to work together and lo and behold a new closeness forms.

So penance is not just about suffering but about hope, healing and happiness and can therefore still have resonance in today's me-me-me world, described in Chapter 1, in which a handbag is likely to be a more pressing preoccupation than heaven and the wealth of celebrity more prized than the welfare of the soul.

Against this background we can now look at the most widely recognised of modern acts of penance: Lent.

8
LENT

The earliest mention of Lent seems to come from the Council of Nicaea in 325 AD, when it was the subject of one of the 20 canons published by that gathering.

The Jesuit and church historian Norman Tanner points out that the word then used for Lent was *tessarakonta*, which is Greek for 40. Until then preparation for Easter was limited to Holy Week and then only in some parts of Christendom. In many other languages the word for Lent is still the same as the word for 40 but the English 'Lent' was chosen because its origin meant to lengthen and as Lent starts the days are lengthening.

However the reference to Lent in the canon concerned is sufficiently passing for it to be clear that this was already a well-established practice and the canon itself makes no reference to the form of its observance other than to call for any disputes in the church to be settled beforehand so that 'the pure Gift may be offered to God after all bitterness has been put away'. This reflects

Christ's command that if we are about to lay a gift upon the altar and remember we have aught against our brother we must first go and be reconciled with him and only then return to make the offering.

Earlier references to preparation for Easter by way of fasting make it clear that there was no uniform observance, but in the immediate period after Nicaea we again catch glimpses of a 40-day period with references to be found in the writings of both St Athanasius and St Cyril of Jerusalem.

Then in the next century we get the clear teaching of Pope St Leo that 'the faithful must fulfil with their fasts the Apostolic institution of the forty days.'

Father William Saunders has observed that the period of 40 days has a long tradition of Biblical significance for it is not only that Christ fasted in the wilderness for 40 days but that Moses stayed with God on Mount Sinai for 40 days and 40 nights and that Elijah walked 40 days and 40 nights to the Mountain of the Lord.

The period being therefore established some time

before the Council of Nicaea, the practice still varied. Father Saunders notes that in Jerusalem Lent lasted eight weeks because Christians fasted for 40 days but excluded both Saturdays and Sundays while in Rome Lent lasted six weeks as people observed each day but Sunday.[1]

Not only the period but the rules varied. In some areas fish was banned as well as meat. St Gregory wrote to St Augustine saying 'we abstain from flesh, meat and from all things that come from flesh, as milk, cheese and eggs.' Vegans would have felt at home. There is some evidence that originally Christians limited themselves to one meal a day but that later a smaller one was added.

Today the rules are few and far between. Ash Wednesday marks the start and Easter Sunday the end. Many Catholics exempt Sundays and the Irish regard St Patrick's day as a no-go area for fast and abstinence. Catholics end their fast after the Easter Vigil on the final Saturday but the Protestants keep going till after the morning service on Easter Sunday.

---

1 Father William Saunders, 'History of Lent', *Arlington Catholic Herald*.

Catholics are expected to refrain from eating meat on Fridays but otherwise Christians simply choose their own penance and it can be as easy or hard as they choose. Our ancestors would have been pretty envious!

First a glance at the above will cry out that the big difference between now and then is that our forebears gave up what is basic whereas we tend to give up luxuries. The all-time favourites for modern Christians when it comes to Lenten penance are: alcohol, chocolates, desserts and meat, none of which are necessary for fuelling our bodies or keeping us alive and the giving up of which we might well want to pursue anyway for reasons of health and waistline.

'Oh,' wailed a parliamentary colleague to me one Lent. 'I so miss twiglets.'

My sympathy quickly dissipated when he added 'Nuts and crisps are just not the same!'

A member of my own family gave up whisky, his favourite drink, and similarly complained that wine and beer were just so boring! I have a feeling the Apostles would have felt a bit bemused.

Yet endurance used to be a *sine qua non* of the Christian life. One of my favourite hymns is *Father Hear the Prayer We Offer*. The opening verse reads:

> Father, hear the prayer we offer,
> Not for ease that prayer shall be,
> But the steep and rugged pathways,
> May we tread rejoicingly.

The curious may read on from the Ancient and Modern Hymnal no. 182.

This hymn emphasises what are increasingly unfashionable Christian virtues – endurance, patience, longsuffering – but it does more than emphasise them. It glorifies them. Here comfort is not sought but dispensed with. 'Not for ease our prayer shall be'. Obstacles are not to be avoided but overcome or, as a later verse puts it, 'but would smite the living fountains from the rocks along our way'. The prayer is not for success but for guidance through 'endeavour, failure, danger'.

In other words this hymn does not subscribe to the view that the Christian way of life is a rosy

121

one, that God will always make it all right and remove all problems, that we can expect to glide through life.

Until fairly recently the concept of endurance – along with its sister virtues of fortitude and self-sacrifice – was fundamental to the Christian philosophy, expressed in the old adage that God tries his saints hard. The history of the church, as earlier observed, gives force to that maxim.

Endurance and fortitude are not virtues with which to sustain only physical suffering or hardship, nor are they merely passive. They are necessary also in guaranteeing mental and moral stamina, powerful weapons in the fight against the desire to give up and have a peaceful life.

Sir Francis Drake prayed:

> *O Lord God, when thou givest to thy*
> *servants to endeavour any great matter,*
> *grant us also to know that it is not the*
> *beginning, but the continuing of the same,*
> *until it be thoroughly finished, which*
> *yieldeth the true glory.*

It was the same spirit which would have kept Wilberforce undeterred in his crucial part in the fight against slavery, a fight which occupied its protagonists for the best part of 40 years.

It is the same spirit which was captured in the Pilgrim's Progress and which has informed the moral of many a lesser work. The Slough of Despond, the Hill of Difficulty and the Valley of Humiliation have little appeal today but Bunyan was writing in an age when fortitude was essential and all but taken for granted. Nor is there much appetite now for taking on all disaster or hobgoblins and foul fiends.

Today in Western Society fortitude is not much valued as a part of everyday life although we still pause to marvel at some outstanding examples of it such as Simon Weston, the Falklands war veteran who was badly burned in action, or children remaining cheerful in the face of disability. We live in the age of the quick-fix solution, of dispensing with rather than working through problems. My grandmother was crippled with arthritis and would have thought a miracle had happened if she had been told she could have a pair of new hips, even if she had to wait years and travel far. Today we regard it as unreasonable if waiting is prolonged and expect local availability, so we promote expectations of fast cures for almost everything.

For the blessing of so much medical and surgical knowledge we must be grateful. It is a gift from God and must therefore not only be used but extended and refined. A greater imperative still is to share it. In half the world science will give you a new heart while in the other half something as basic as an impacted wisdom tooth can render every day a ceaseless misery of pain.

The downside however is a creeping conviction that nothing or – more sinister – nobody should exist for which or for whom cures are not available. It is no longer a person's right to endure a quality of life rejected by the more fortunate.

Hence 'not for resuscitation' appears in the hospital notes of disabled people. A life-saving operation may be denied to a Downs child which would be available to its mentally competent counterpart. The unborn may never be born if they have cleft palate or club foot. Beyond a certain age life itself can be denied.

Yet how dare anyone decide for another that he or she is unequal to the burden or to the time of trial? Beethoven was deaf, Milton blind. From the confines of a wheelchair Professor Stephen Hawking bestrides the world with brilliance. They and many others have smitten the rocks in their path and sent living fountains gushing forth.

Quick-fix solutions: lunchtime abortion, quickie divorce, instant credit, nothing acts faster than Anadin, lose a stone in a fortnight.

The harvest which mankind now seeks from the earth is an instant one. It does not need sowing and nurturing and reaping. It must be there, ready, rich, tasty whenever and wherever anyone wants it.

Insidiously but with huge speed the people of the developed world have come to rely on this life as having all the answers.

It is not surprising that our ancestors found such appeal in the concept of eternal rest. The daily struggle, hard toil for little reward, the pain of child mortality, the crippling, depressing force of disease, the harshness of the law, sadly also the harshness of the church and its judgements made their journey on this earth a vale of tears. Their hopes were vested in the world to come, where scripture taught all wrongs would be avenged and all inequalities would be reversed, where the poor would find rest in Abraham's bosom and the rich would envy them from afar (see the parable of Dives and Lazarus, Lk. 16.19–25).

Yet the concept of endurance is not merely about bearing with a good grace the misfortunes life throws at us. It is also about self-sacrifice and the deliberate mortification of the flesh. With convents and monasteries closing for lack of vocations and candidates for the priesthood (especially the celibate priesthood of the Roman Catholic Church) in decline, we may deduce a growing unwillingness to practise self-denial in this life in the hope of salvation in the next.

Lent is widely ignored and pilgrimages, if made at all, tend to take place in comfortable, air-conditioned coaches. Fasting, thirsting, long treks, and foot blisters indicate not dedication but obsession, according to modern mores. Furthermore the end of some pilgrimages is undedifying as one arrives not at a holy place, remote and silent, but in a whirl of commercialism. Lourdes has a good line in peddling holy water but the worst of all is the church of the Holy Sepulchre and Our Lord's alleged birthplace in Bethlehem, where queues of pilgrims kiss 'the very spot on which the manger lay'.

Rot. After two millennia of very chequered history and development the Virgin herself couldn't locate the stable never mind the precise placing of the manger. As for the church of the Holy Sepulchre, I doubt very much if that is the precise location of His resurrection but even if it is His spirit will have departed long ago from such a den of dispute and profit-making. Holy place, my foot! It's just another tourist attraction.

No wonder visitors arrive in coaches rather than on foot.

It is however encouraging that walking or cycling the Pilgrim Way to Compostela is regaining popularity, and some sturdy pilgrims walk to Rome, though usually for charitable sponsorship rather than only for the good of the soul.

Does it matter? Have we really lost anything by devaluing stoicism? So what if we give up the steep and rugged pathway and opt instead for a life in green pastures? Does it really take us further from God if we studiously avoid the rocks rather than smite them?

Consider St Paul: 'I have fought the good fight, I have finished my course, I have kept the faith' (2 Tim. 4.7).

He knew endeavour, failure, danger. But we do not always need to look to the distant past or to martyrdom. Terry Waite, the Archbishop of Canterbury's envoy who was held hostage by Jihadists, faced over four years in captivity a trial of faith and endurance. So did Karol Wojtyla, now better known as Pope John Paul II, as he resisted first nazism and then communism and the habit remained as he pushed himself to the limit with every fresh tour undertaken against declining health and vigour, smiting rock after rock. Would they have grown as close to God had they endured less? If the answer to that is 'no' then it follows that our faith grows and flourishes when it is tested.

Christ told us it was easier for a camel to pass through the eye of a needle than for a rich man to enter the Kingdom of Heaven but it was not the possession of money he was condemning. He was condemning the hold which money and ease can take. The rich young man who wanted to follow Him could not face giving up his life of comfort, trading a soft bed for the hard ground, not even for eternal life would he forsake green pastures.

The Christian life demands self-sacrifice. Giving is only true giving if it hurts. A fiver casually deposited in the collection plate is not giving if it comes from an income of £50,000. Five minutes chatting to a lonely person is not time given to others if we happened to be standing at the bus stop anyway. Similarly the Christian life demands the self-sacrifice of endurance: enduring ridicule and not compromising, keeping on – and on and on – with a seemingly hopeless but just cause, never forsaking it, never taking the easy way out, praying when we are tired out; relieving the burdens of others before our own, fighting wrongdoing and not being satisfied till we have overcome it, always keeping the faith until we have finished our course. Not only travelling the extra mile, but also actively seeking out the opportunity to do so.

For obvious reasons we think of Calvary when we think of the sacrifice of Christ. As great a test of endurance however was Gethsemane. Alone, with everyone else flopped out in sleep, He steeled himself to what lay ahead and embraced it. He drew close to His father in those terrible few hours.

Great exigencies can produce great courage, sometimes exhibited in very simple ways. Victor Klemperer records in his diaries how a German once crossed the street to speak to him in the height of the Nazi persecution. Klemperer told him to go away, that it was dangerous to speak to a Jew, but the German stood his ground saying 'I can't do anything else'.

It echoes Luther's comment, 'I can do no other' (referred to in Chapter 6).

But we can all imagine what the families and friends of those men would say. Perhaps the German's wife wept and pleaded and said, 'Think of your family, think of us. Don't do it. Help the Jews secretly but don't go up to them in the street.' Or Luther's friends 'Look, don't. There are other ways, less dangerous ways.'

The imperative for both however was too great. They had to keep the faith and were prepared to endure the consequences.

Perhaps the reason that sacrifice and fortitude are out of fashion is because we do not feel the great imperative: that of earning eternal rest, of not stirring up God's wrath, of avoiding eternal damnation. The real attraction of the green pastures is the fond belief that the steep and rugged pathway leads nowhere in the end and the rocks are someone else's problem. In other words you can have it all – in this world and the next. Christ taught us quite the opposite and His teaching of the judgement is consistent: Dives and Lazarus; the man who buried his talent in the ground; the wheat and the chaff; weeping and wailing and gnashing of teeth. And that is but a small selection.

Yet the imperative to avoid being on the wrong side of it has all but disappeared and with it the imperative to put ourselves regularly to the test and to will ourselves to endure it.

131

The catechism of the Catholic Church sums up the fate which awaits us all:

> Death puts an end to human life as the time open to either accepting or rejecting the divine grace manifested in Christ. The New Testament speaks of judgement primarily in its aspect of the final encounter with Christ in his second coming, but also repeatedly affirms that each will be rewarded immediately after death in accordance with his works and faith. The parable of the poor man Lazarus and the words of Christ on the cross to the good thief, as well as other New Testament texts, speak of a final destiny of the soul – a destiny which can be different for some and for others.
>
> Each man receives his eternal retribution in his immortal soul at the very moment of his death, in a particular judgement that refers his life to Christ: either entrance into the blessedness of heaven or immediate and everlasting damnation.'

Once that would have been sufficient imperative to start smiting the rocks!

Of course this all refers to the direction and priorities of our lives rather than to the 40 days of Lent but Lent is now used by many as a test of will rather than as a penance. It is in many ways a recognition that we do indeed seek out the green pastures and we are curious to see if we can stand a small sojourn on the steep and rugged pathway. Perhaps it is churlish to point out that the hymn assumes us to do so *rejoicingly* rather than grudgingly.

St Paul actively rejoiced in his thorn in the flesh. Whatever this physical malaise was he asked Christ three times to remove it and the Lord did not oblige. The effect of this he describes in one of his epistles to the Corinthians.

> *And so to keep me from being unduly elated*
> *by the magnificence of such revelations, I*
> *was given a sharp pain in my body which*
> *came as Satan's messenger to bruise me; this*
> *was to save me from being unduly elated.*
> *Three times I begged the Lord to rid me of*
> *it, but His answer was 'My grace is all you*

need; power comes to its full strength in weakness'. I shall therefore prefer to find my joy and pride in the very things that are my weakness; and then the power of Christ will come and rest upon me. Hence I am well content, for Christ's sake, with weakness, contempt, persecution, hardship, and frustration; for when I am weak then I am strong. (New English Bible).

The Authorised version puts it even more strongly than 'well content': *Therefore I take pleasure in infirmities, in reproaches, in necessities, in persecutions, in distresses for Christ's sake.*

Whether content or taking pleasure is the more accurate translation is best left to scholars but the essence is clear: St Paul welcomed his particular penance which to a lesser mortal would have been galling when all around him were so many incidences of healing.

St Paul however had the advantage of being one of the most significant saints in Christian history. What about the rest of us poor fish? Can penance ever be a pleasure? Can it really cause us to rejoice?

Ask any Marathon runner how he feels at the end of the race. He is unlikely to be other than exultant, delighted, enthused. But what about during the race, when his legs are aching, the sweat is soaking his track suit, his breathing is painful and there is still a distance of ten miles to cover? How does he feel then? Is he rejoicing?

The answer is probably yes. He has set himself a task, he knows he is being tested and he is enjoying the effort even if he will be glad when it is all over for another year.

Those who stay the course in Lent probably feel much the same…er … pleased with themselves. Oh, dear. That is not the idea at all.

As the Easter Vigil approaches signalling the end of Lent I and most people I know are counting down the days. As the bells ring out the Gloria and the penitential season passes there is always a tiny element of self-congratulation: *I did it! I didn't slip up once.*

Well, it's only human but there are other ways in which penance can make us joyful, even if it hardly fills us with a sense of fun.

9

Lent And Doubt

Penance can bring us closer to God because it focuses our attention on him. Or at least it should do. A good way of illustrating this is to look at the Catholic practice of refraining from meat on Fridays.

At school I hated Fridays because we always seemed to have cheese pie for lunch. Supper was better because we often had fish and chips but lunch was ghastly cheese pie. I suppose now we would call it a quiche but it consisted of nothing but cheese, enlivened by not even a hint of tomato, and it tasted horrible.

What I was meant to think at Friday lunch was: 'I am now going to commemorate Our Lord's passion by refraining from eating flesh and blood.' Instead what I thought was 'Oh, hell, cheese pie again.'

The first of those thoughts has the potential for joy but the second has only the promise of misery. Penance on its own does not focus our thoughts on God, but a consciousness of why we are doing it does.

The greater the faith the happier the penitent but penance can sometimes be a way of enhancing faith so let us briefly consider the role of faith's apparent opposite: doubt. Today that might conjure up an image of a believer disturbed by the arguments of Dawkins but we find it in unlikely places such as the hearts of some of the greatest biblical heroes.

The obvious is, of course, Doubting Thomas. The famous incident in St John's gospel has entered the lexicon and 2,000 years later this saint and martyr is associated principally with his famous declaration that he would not believe the resurrection until he could put his hands in the wounds. *I'll believe it when I see it*, is how we would render his reaction in modern parlance.

The scene when he does that and proclaims the risen Christ 'my Lord and my God' has inspired many artists with its drama.

Yet this is but one of many examples of doubt from the Bible. To have doubts is a natural function of the human psyche. People in love doubt they are worthy of that love being reciprocated; strivers doubt whether they will ever reach their goals; the most innocent of accused men may doubt if he will prove that innocence. We doubt the weather forecast and politicians' promises. Doubt is a natural product of having to make judgements about anything that is not visible or audible or of a tangible form.

So some of the greatest biblical heroes had doubt but interestingly God's reaction varied enormously and that is often the unexamined aspect of doubt in the Bible.

Let us begin with Moses. Any politician would have some sympathy with Moses, who was implored by the children of Israel to get them out of Egypt and then when the Promised Land did not immediately materialise turned on him and said they would have been better off in Egypt. They were angry and fractious and now they were also desperate because there was no water. God told Moses to take them up to a specified rock from which He would cause water to pour.

Imagine the scene: the crowd has been promised water and there they all are standing at the rock waiting for it and nothing happens. They look from the rock to Moses and from Moses to the rock and nothing happens. And one can imagine what the suspense does. They begin to mutter, certain they have been misled, as they all look at a perfectly ordinary rock doing nothing except be the lump of stone it has always been.

And one can imagine Moses feeling increasingly embarrassed and suddenly doubtful. So he strikes the rock. Let he who has never tapped a television set to encourage it to perform cast the first stone. But God is sufficiently angry to deny Moses entry to the Promised Land, a severe penance if ever there was one.

That may seem all rather alarming. Is doubt really so terrible? Could a doubting heart negate a small penance being voluntarily undertaken? Should I give up Lent if I have doubts?

For reassurance we should look at Gideon. The angel of the Lord appeared to him and said 'The Lord is with thee'. And what does Gideon reply? The Hebrew equivalent of 'Oh, yeah?' He demands to know why, if the Lord is with the Israelites, they are suffering at the hands of their enemies. And where are all the miracles He used to do?

God does not, so to speak, take offence. He doesn't say 'Here is an angel. Is not that proof enough?' Instead he patiently explains that He has chosen Gideon to deliver his fellow countrymen from their enemies. But still Gideon is beset by doubt and actually asks God for a sign that He really is speaking to him. So God arranges a fairly spectacular display of fire from a rock but even that is not enough. He actually asks God not only to send a sign but presumes to specify what it must be: he will put out a fleece and asks that next day the fleece be soaking wet but the ground around it dry. God obliges. And that's not enough. Now just to be absolutely certain, one angel, one fire and one wet fleece later, that it is not all coincidence and imagination he asks God to do the reverse and give him a dry fleece and wet ground. And God does.

So, two very different responses to doubt in the Old Testament. Now let us turn to the New and

141

to Zachary, a just man whose works are pleasing to the Lord, and whose wife Elizabeth is barren. One day Gabriel appears to him and tells him Elizabeth will conceive. He doesn't believe it and asks how it can possibly be so when his wife has been barren for years.

For Zachary there is no fire from the rock, no miracles with fleeces, only a hefty dose of divine anger as God strikes him dumb for the duration of the pregnancy, saying it is because he doubted the word of the Lord.

So doubt angers God? Not with Thomas. He is actually encouraged to test the resurrection for himself by feeling the wounds.

The reactions are different in these four examples because the men concerned were at different stages in their spiritual lives and the clear message is that we are not expected to be in a state of certainty from the moment we believe, are not expected to dispense with doubt, that faith does not collapse the moment a small niggle attenuates it. Indeed the message is that God can use doubt, that it is a tool of our maturing in faith not an obstacle to it.

So let's compare Moses and Gideon. Moses had walked with God for a very long time and God had never let him down. Moses had seen it all: the burning bush, the plagues of Egypt, the staff turning into a serpent, the parting of the red seas. He had heard the voice of God literally. The children of Israel had been extracted from difficulty after difficulty with manna from Heaven and flocks of quails just two examples. In short Moses had been delivered proof after proof of God's faithfulness, had himself been favoured by God above other men, was charged with a sacred trust, was given authority by God Himself. By the time the grumbling tribes arrived at the rock there should no longer have been any room for any doubt at all.

But Gideon was in a very different position. He was being plucked from obscurity to defeat the Midianites and must have been beset by doubts and fears. He was at the beginning of his walk with God, his faith in his mission at an early stage and the doubts that he had were part of his journey to fulfil that mission.

It is not fanciful to imagine Gideon looking back in later years and saying 'Whatever was I thinking, to keep asking for signs like that? That business with the fleece! Why did God put up with it?' It is a comforting image: whatever doubts we have now we can look forward to a time when they will have gone.

So now we come to the New Testament and Zachary. We are told that both he and his wife were 'righteous before God, walking in all the commandments, blameless' and that they were of advanced years. So they had walked with the Lord a long time, Zachary held priestly office and now here was Gabriel himself. He had reached a stage where he was expected to trust and so God was not pleased when he failed.

Thomas of course had at first glance advantages not shared by Zachary. He would have seen some of the miracles at first hand and had accompanied Christ Himself but he had of course also seen the arrest and crucifixion and would have known of the burial. And he wasn't doubting an angel of the Lord but rather the excited babble of his bewildered fellow humans. All the evidence is that the real test of the early Christians was just beginning, that they were about to be left on their own and facing a journey very different

144

from that involved in travelling the country with a crowd-pulling miracle worker. So, whatever they may have seen in the past, they were now at a very early and vulnerable stage of their journey with God.

So more is expected of us as we grow. But God uses doubt and we often forget that. We pray 'O, Lord, I believe. Help Thou my unbelief.' Yet we can also pray 'Use and bless my unbelief.'

Let us look at our four examples again. Moses. There would have been those in the crowd who saw the doubt on Moses' face, who thought 'even the gaffer wasn't sure that time' and who would remember that next time and be more receptive to promises. Gideon. In future years he could always say to any admirer who thought his faith perfect and his own pathetic 'Oh, once I looked upon the angel of the Lord and still had doubts.'

Zachary's dumbness prepared people for the baby being something very special. That Elizabeth was expecting may have been a miracle in its own right but that strange affliction added to the mystery that was to be John the Baptist.

And Thomas, whose very name is synonymous with doubt? That rational mortal whose reaction to the wild tales of his companions was probably exactly what our own would have been? Who probably said to the women full of what they had seen at the tomb the first century equivalent of 'calm down, dears'.

The fruits of his doubt lie in the message which rings down to us across two millennia: Blessed are they who have not seen and yet believed. That is our call, our challenge and our comfort. The greatest servants of God have doubted, even those who had already put Him to the test and for them as for us doubt can be a positive influence.

Faith is a great gift of God and so is reason. If occasionally they collide it is because they must exist as one not as things apart and unreconcilable and it is the moment of reconciliation of faith and reason which defeats doubt.

You cannot be courageous unless you are first afraid for without fear no courage is required and you cannot have faith without doubt for without doubt where is the need for faith? To be without doubt is to deny ourselves the joy of that moment of realisation in which we can say, with Thomas, my Lord and my God.

So penance can be for the doubter as much as for the already faithful. 'I don't do Lent' can become 'What can Lent do for me?'

10

THE JOY OF LENT

Lent, as I have observed in Chapter 8, can be not merely challenging but joyful. The real joy is that it can bring us closer to God and that includes the times when we fail either through a moment's forgetfulness or from weakness. When this happens we should treat it as we would treat a lapse during a diet: not as an excuse to abandon the attempt, but as a regrettable interlude between succeeding and succeeding. After all if one lapses as much as a dozen times during Lent that still leaves 28 days of success and has the additional merit of not leaving one feeling smug and self-congratulatory as the Gloria rings out on Easter Sunday or in the case of Catholics during the Easter Vigil on the final Saturday.

We talk of prayer and fasting, but fasting is itself a type of prayer, as it reminds us of the presence of God and of our relationship with Him. Every time we refuse the thing we have given up or carry out the act we have pledged or donate the extra alms we have promised we are saying 'This is for You. It is because Your son gave up so much for me. Sorry it's a bit pathetic by comparison.'

We are also bearing witness to Him and we should not be embarrassed by this aspect of it. How often have we heard somebody say that he can't refuse a glass of champagne at a wedding because people might think it odd. Christ Himself was thought pretty odd and was frowned upon by those who adhered to the social norms of first century Jerusalem. He feasted with publicans and sinners, was dubbed a glutton and a wine-bibber, broke the Sabbath, drove long-established merchants out of the Temple and verbally roasted the authorities.

Certainly He knew what it was to let down others' expectations, as already described when looking at the crucifixion.

After that letting down the person who expects us to abandon Lent for special occasions seems a bit tame but the whole point of Lent is that we are following Christ's example in very small ways. We are not off to the desert for 40 days without food or water but we can refuse some kinds of food and drink. We are not preparing to die horribly but we are trying to suffer just a tiny bit. We are not causing horrid fear and despair to our family and friends but we are prepared to defy a few conventions whether they approve or not and these small efforts bring us closer to Him.

The essence of feeling close to God is communicating with Him and listening to Him talking to us. In worldly terms communication has never been so easy. Once, if a relative or friend had emigrated to Australia, the only means of communication would have been a letter sent by sea and received many weeks later; then it became possible to send such letters by air and to make telephone calls to the other side of the world. Now we have instant communication by email and can talk to each other on Skype.

Our prayer journey is very similar. When we begin praying God can seem far away and communication very uncertain. This is as true for the believer as for the doubter but as we persevere it all gets quicker, easier and more effective. Only time and effort can prove this and if anyone refuses to try then he cannot find this out.

Basil Hume, the late Cardinal Archbishop of Westminster, who was also a monk of Ampleforth Abbey, wrote that the spiritual life and prayer are almost interchangeable words, that without prayer there can be no serious spiritual life. But he was not talking so much about prayer as in a formal address to God as about meditation.

Therefore upping one's prayer effort in Lent is not saying that prayer is itself a penance to be endured through extra worship but rather it seeks to enhance our relationship with God, which is why we have embarked upon Lent in the first place.

Prayer can indeed compensate for much of our Lenten endurance because it can be joyful. We need not think only in terms of Calvary but in terms of the resurrection and can eagerly look forward to it in our conversations with Him. We can think of the Apostles enjoying Palm Sunday as often as we think of them, hurt and baffled, staring uncomprehendingly at their hero on the cross. We can picture the women creeping to the tomb on that fateful morning and smile at what is to come.

Lent however is more than just a preparation for Easter even though it comes immediately before that celebration in the Christian calendar. If it came before Christmas or after Easter or after the Ascension it would still serve much the same function: to allow us to say sorry and draw nearer to the One Whose death redeemed us and sensing his forgiveness would still bring us joy. Of course the fact that Advent is also supposed to be a penitential season in preparation for Christmas is conveniently overlooked or forgotten in more secular preparations for the season of over-indulgence.

Probably only true saints actively enjoy or look forward to the sacrifices of Lent but the season can bring its own joy for the rest of us: contentment, closeness to God and a sense of having tried for His sake.

The Christian martyrs went to their deaths with a variety of emotions: fear, determination and, yes, joy. They were certain of their cause, certain of the Heaven they were about to enter, certain that no life on this earth was worth trading for it. They had fought the good fight, they had kept the faith, they had finished their course. We can obtain a tiny glimpse of that reassurance through Lenten observance and indeed through any act of penance. If it brings us closer to God then it brings us also closer to Heaven.

We are fighting the good fight and keeping the faith and if we veer off course with the odd bit of chocolate we can get back on course again.

We should also consider not only Christ but His betrayer. The sin of Judas was less the treachery than the despair: instead of believing that he could be forgiven and join the other Apostles in his Master's kingdom, he thought all was lost and killed himself. It would have been better, said Christ, that Judas had never been born.

That teaches us two things: first to see lapses in proportion and secondly never just to give up because we have fallen off the straight and narrow. The early Apostles were after all what in modern parlance would be called a right shower.

St Peter was a coward and a foul-mouthed liar, cursing and swearing as he insisted he had never known the Nazarene. Saints James and John were vainglorious, arguing away about who would be the more important in the Kingdom of Heaven. Nathaniel was a right old snob, asking if any good could come out of Galilee. Yet this unpromising bunch was the choice of God for the foundation of his Church.

And they certainly didn't let Him down. St Peter is proof enough. He alone had the guts to follow when Jesus was led away but his courage was not proof against the prospect of a similar fate so he lied desperately when challenged and then, appalled by his action, went out and wept bitterly. Years later, as a result of his preaching and conversions, he was crucified upside down (he did not think he was worthy to be crucified in the same way as Christ) by a vengeful Rome.

Let us now translate that into the rather more prosaic experiences of the modern western Christian. We form a resolution, we can't quite stick to it, we repent of our failure, we find a fresh flow of resolution, then we carry on for Him renewed, re-invigorated and joyful.

There are, of course, still parts of the world where to be a Christian can yet be to court trial and death and many lesser forms of persecution. It

155

can help to remember that when we are regarding the trivial temptations of a western Lent.

In the above example of St Peter, the major role played by repentance should be noted. This, as stated in earlier chapters, is the precursor of penance: sin must not only be acknowledged but earnestly repented. It was the beginning of the process which turned St Peter from coward to martyr.

Today we often forget that the Church is first and foremost for sinners, that they are the *raison d'etre* of its existence. Christ did not choose the 12 bravest and holiest men He could find.

Consider what a shocking character St Paul was, persecuting the Christians, fighting the Church at every turn, egging on those who killed St Stephen, terrorising the faithful. Then he took the road to Damascus and the rest is history but it is significant how in his writings St Paul repents, calling himself the least of the disciples at a time when he was travelling the world for Christ. Yet Paul was always rejoicing in Christ and in salvation.

It has been noted earlier that both Church

and State consider that sins or crimes offend in themselves as well as against the individual victims. As pointed out in Chapter 5, however, a major difference is that when the Church forgives it does not hold a person's past record against him, whereas the State will keep a criminal's misdeeds on record and use that effectively to prevent him from finding certain types of employment. Convictions will not be 'spent' until a substantial period of time after the crime was not only committed but also expiated. Calvary washed away sin and Paul, once accepted, was accepted as if he had never persecuted the Church. There is thus a special dimension to Christian repentance for the forgiveness is absolute, not conditional.

The joy of Lent is then in essence the joy of repentance which is the precursor to God's forgiveness and thence to the assurance of Heaven. In that it does not differ from any other act of penance but it is different in requiring a sustained penance over a period of time which, unlike imposed penance, we are at liberty to break any time we choose.

The joy of Lent is also that it is an act not only of

penance but of prayer and, as with any prayer, the joy is that it brings us closer to God.

We might pause to consider here that the one time when penance is almost second nature is childhood, that time of innocence and rejoicing in small things. The average adult, rebuking a small child, will take him or her through all the stages of penance.

'Johnny, that was wrong. Say sorry to Jenny and give her back her toy. Don't do it again.'

In that one all too familiar sentence we have: recognition of wrongdoing, confession of fault, atonement and amendment of life. Children expect no less and would feel insecure – if temporarily relieved – were such admonition not forthcoming.

When the toy is returned and Jenny smiles it is all over and usually Johnny is soon smiling too, a small joy from a small penance.

In purely human terms of course the joy of Lent is when it is over so we must ask, what next? Anybody who has endured a period of debilitating illness or acute anxiety will know the joy when it is all over of throwing oneself back into life. Lent is rather less dramatic but just as the recovering patient or reassured worrier will take some lessons, some residue of the experience with him so will the penitent emerging from Lent.

11

THANKS BE IT IS ALL OVER

What comes after penance? After Lent? After the period of self-imposed or involuntary penance is over? After the prisoner walks away from the gates? As we have seen in an earlier chapter sometimes the penance can produce a new way of life or a new dimension to it. The heavy drinker discovers the pleasures of sobriety, the man doing community service carries on in a voluntary capacity, the believer who has committed more time to prayer continues with the new pattern. These examples constitute amendment of life after penance, which is a normal aftermath, but where the penance has been spiritually inspired, as in Lent, the amendment of life can be greater closeness to God.

Lent particularly can be a penance perceived in isolation as people go back with relish to whatever it was they gave up, until the next year's Lent produces an imperative to put oneself to the test again. Between the two penance becomes short-lived episodes of response to specific sins but the concept of voluntarily enduring a demanding period of it is put on hold until next time.

Yet consciousness of sin as opposed to a specific wrongdoing is a part of the daily walk with God and therefore it is arguable that regular penance will bring us closer to Him. Certainly that was what many monastic orders thought and even today Opus Dei thinks and the methods they devised could be brutal. It takes a lot of believing that the Lord who gives us a healthy, functioning body wants us to damage it regularly in His name.

There are however less dramatic forms of penance and some Christians find a daily penitential act helpful whether of self-deprivation, greater time given to others or enhanced almsgiving. The penance will vary rather than be carried out to a set pattern as in Lent but it will be a conscious act of contrition rather than just a fleeting urge to be good.

Does that mean that Lent should be forgotten? Or is there a way of carrying its joy through the year until Easter next looms? Its *joy*, not its prescribed penance?

Earthly joys are many and of different orders of magnitude. We rejoice when we fall in love, have children, recover from serious illness and also when we win £5 on the lottery or catch the train with seconds to spare. The quality of the joy varies enormously but it is a normal aspect of being human that, except when we are in deepest anxiety, gloom or pain we will find countless causes of either sustained or fleeting joy in our lives.

The Christian life is the same. We can thank God for a small flower blooming, a cat purring or the safe return of a loved one who has been through danger. We will certainly be more thankful for the last than the first but even the smallest act of thanksgiving will be joyful.

If Lent has brought us closer to God in the ways discussed in the last chapter then we can continue, consciously, to hang on to that closeness, through enhanced prayer, the occasional revisiting of the penance and the sense of God in our daily lives. This last is more than just thanking Him or saying sorry to Him in those moments when we have sudden cause.

For some, prayer is at first difficult and people

163

can initially feel they are speaking into a void. For others, the concept of God is so great that it can appear impossible to begin to address Him. The following paragraphs may appear to trivialise the exercise for those who are past this point, but I hope they will help the hesitant.

We often stay close to departed loved ones by remembering not our emotions but theirs. We plant their favourite roses, recall their favourite sayings, think in the middle of some event how much they would have loved it or laughed at it.

The reverse is also true as we imagine their pain. 'Thank God your father is not here to see this day.' 'Poor Gran would have been heartbroken.' 'Whatever would Jack have said had he been here?' 'It's a good job they didn't try this in Mary's time!' 'I wish Harry were still around. He would have sorted this lot out.'

We can think in the same way of Christ Himself. Instead of saying 'what a lovely display the roses are this year. Thank you, Lord,' we can say 'You would have loved these when You were here. They are even better than the lilies of the field!' That in turn will probably produce reflections about spinning and reaping and may even influence some decision we are taking or cause us to pause in some extravagance or indulgence but, crucially, imagining Christ on earth, can bring us closer than thinking of Him as a Spirit in Heaven. We are not yet familiar with Heaven but we understand Earth only too well.

Lent is a time when we do focus on Christ as man as well as God, fasting, praying, wanting to escape fate then accepting that fate, feeling pain at betrayal and desertion. The loneliness of the desert. Gethsemane. Calvary. Courage. Resignation. Terrible pain. Letting everyone down. Only at the resurrection does he re-appear to us as God.

Yet because He is indeed God we can feel, if only subconsciously, that is the only way to think of Him. Of course He is with us every moment as God but thinking of him as a man on earth and how he would have reacted brings Him very close.

'You would have understood that, because that was how You reacted to such and such,' can bring us closer than 'I know you understand'

165

simply because the first requires an act of imagination as well as a focus on the relevant part of the Gospels.

Infinite Goodness is a concept. A good man is something we have all encountered. Mystics apart, we can therefore relate more easily to the second and sometimes we should not aim for such lofty holiness in the way we approach casual prayer.

Suppose we feel a bit hungry. We can of course remember the fasting in the desert or the sufferings of the Third World and reflect, rightly, that we have no cause to complain. We can even offer it up. But we will still feel a bit hungry.

We can, however, also say to God: 'You understand hunger – you made breakfast on the shore for Your disciples, when they had been fishing all night.'

If we pray in that fashion we will still feel hungry but not so guilty about it and because we have just effectively told ourselves that He would have understood and given us a bite to eat had He been around, we feel closer to him. It is not just that we ask Him to understand us but we understand Him.

Holiness is wonderful but because it is a state the Christian desires and aspires to reach it can seem remote. By definition something which we aspire to is not yet within our grasp. Looking at pictures of the Virgin, all serene, with angelic child in her arms complete with halo and cherubic smile is fine, but imagining the reality of a hassled woman perched upon a donkey, dusty from a long journey, with a teething baby crying for food and a weary, footsore husband brings us closer. The first requires an exercise in imagination but the second is instantly familiar and we identify with the familiar.

So for the faithful the spiritual efforts and rewards of Lent can be carried on all year round but if Lent is also for the doubter what happens to him afterwards?, to the latter day Thomases who, not having put their fingers in the wounds, endured Lent but without the concomitant commitment that makes it bearable for most of us? Those who are never going to find Gabriel on their doorstep but who want to find God – if he is there, they would quickly add?

Often the enlightenment comes a little later, some weeks perhaps after the penance and the prayers to Him Who mayest be there are nothing more than memories. Gradually, now that he is chomping away merrily upon the chocolates or sinking down into an armchair clutching a G and T complete with ice and slice, the doubter becomes aware that something is missing, some closeness that was beginning to warm his life has disappeared. What was it? Oh, yes, God. So perhaps he tries again with a quick prayer.

In the evangelical tradition, conversion is always a specific moment as in the case of Paul. There is a point where you ask the Lord into your heart and are born again, but for others conversion is a very long path with many significant points along the way passing almost unnoticed. The growth of belief is gradual, the loss of unbelief a slow erosion rather than a sudden explosion. There is no one second when the convert says 'this is when it happened'. Instead one day he just notices that it already has.

Penance in its many forms, including but not exclusively Lent, can take someone along that hidden path and can certainly start one upon it. But Lent is by definition a limited period of time. It requires no permanent deprivation. Doubtless the rich young man who refused Christ's request to sell all that he had and follow Him would have been only too glad to give it up for 40 days if he knew he could go back to his wealth and possessions at the end of them. One of the motivations for keeping going in Lent is precisely that it will not last for ever.

Yet for some penance is never over, whether it is the imposed sentence of a whole-life imprisonment or the voluntary vows of poverty, chastity and obedience taken by nuns and monks or in the case of the second vow the Catholic priest. Then there are the vows taken by others which end up lasting a lifetime.

One of the most remarkable women I have known was Phyllis Bowman, the anti-abortion campaigner who, despite major difficulties in breathing, was still dictating letters on her deathbed when she passed away in her eighties. In 1967, when abortion was first made legal, Phyllis took a vow to abstain from alcohol until the law was reversed.

169

The vow was a mixture of penance and 'offering it up', a modern equivalent of the sackcloth and ashes designed to appease an angry Deity. The penance was on behalf of humanity in general for the deaths of so many unborn children (over seven million by the time Phyllis died) but the abstinence was also designed to enhance the pleas to God for intervention, as is always the fasting in prayer and fasting.

Phyllis never did have another drink.

Whether or not Profumo intended the rest of his life to be devoted to Toynbee Hall, that was how it turned out and the life he left behind had no charms with which to lure him back.

Those in monastic orders similarly live a life of penance. How else can one describe denying oneself at the outset any chance of normal family life, giving up all wordly possessions and staggering out of bed at dawn each day to sing lauds? Some even give up the right to chat to each other and spend their days in penitential silence.

Here the self-denial has several purposes: to be a penance for one's own sins but also for those of the world in general; to enhance prayer (vast quantities of it) and to promote closeness to God with whom they intercede on behalf of the rest of us, who are usually just too busy.

The parish priest who has chosen chastity will live a more normal life than the nun or monk in closed orders but his penance will sometimes be harder to endure because he is surrounded by the normal sources of temptation. The aid-worker who is constrained by no vows at all will often find a life of self-imposed poverty in the third world tougher than any Trappist monk's because it is so easy to walk away from it. In other words the greater the temptation the greater the penance.

The early Christians eagerly devoted their lives to spreading the message, which was easier in some parts of the world than in others. If they suffered for it then like St Paul they rejoiced and many did indeed suffer lifelong persecution or lives cut short by a punitive State.

Closeness to God through prayer and penance can sometimes be almost tangible. We know when we meet it in other people. In the course of my entire life I have encountered it in its purest

171

form – a sense of being closer to God just by being with that person – fewer than half a dozen times.

The search for closeness to God is admirably summed up by one of those people, the late Cardinal Hume:

> *Now it is a fact that my spiritual life is more a wandering in Blunderland than a resting and relaxing in Wonderland. I would guess that most of us would say the same of ourselves.... What matters, however, is that minds and hearts should be involved in the search for God, where the seeking and the finding go hand in hand. It is the process of getting to know God and learning to love Him. It is intimacy with Him that we seek. We try to go beyond every experience of knowledge and love, which we have now, to another experience, which is beyond our grasp but not entirely out of our reach.*[1]

---

1 Cardinal Hume, *Basil in Blunderland* (London: Darton, Longman and Todd, 1977).

In addition to Basil Hume, Pope John Paul II and, to a lesser extent, Mother Teresa of Calcutta made me feel nearer to God. But two of the charity workers in my constituency, Pat McCabe and Pat Wilmshurst, always caused me to think whenever I met them *and for His dwelling and His throne.* Significantly all had either given up a great deal, chosen to live very simply or suffered themselves in the course of a lifetime's unwavering devotion to Christ. It is as if penance were second nature to them.

Penance is not usually second nature to those on whom it has been imposed by the State but there are many examples of people finding prison a cleansing experience, notably Jonathan Aitken who fell from being a cabinet minister to a prison lavatory cleaner but who turned this uncongenial episode in his life into a source of spiritual renewal. All prison chaplains have heart-warming tales to relate of offenders, sometimes even murderers, finding God in prison and continuing to grow in the faith outside it but by and large those who have to be there do not want to be and do not embrace the penance.

The late Lord Longford used to claim that Myra

Hindley had undergone a genuine conversion when she became a Catholic but she campaigned all her life to be released, thereby rejecting the notion of a lifelong penance. Those who reject penance can never find its comfort or joy.

12

PENANCE AFTER DEATH

Anybody coming out of Lent knows that there is life after penance but is there penance after life?

Laying aside the afterlife for a moment we may still find examples of punishment inflicted after death. There is the obvious fictional one of Michael Henchard in the *Mayor of Casterbridge*. His will stipulated that his daughter be not troubled with news of his death, that no bell toll, that he be not buried in consecrated ground, that no mourners walk behind his coffin, that no flowers be put on his grave and that no man remember him. Even by Hardy's standards that is pretty gloomy.

Henchard had done great wrong in his life and this was his way of recognising it. As he could not know what was happening, the penance lay in wishing this on himself while still living but there have been real cases of attempts to punish the dead through dishonour and disgrace.

Charles II, normally the most relaxed of monarchs, could never forgive the regicides for the death of his father so after his restoration he had Cromwell dug up, executed and his head put on display. Ugh! Presumably this both relieved Charles' long-held anger and grief and also made the point that Cromwell was a traitor. For centuries the Church refused to bury those who had committed suicide in consecrated ground and more recently we have seen Jimmy Savile's elaborate headstone removed, although that was probably as much to prevent desecration as it was a mark of shame.

In all these cases only the reputation could suffer not the dead body. So what about the soul?

In 1769 James Boswell asked Samuel Johnson 'What do you think, Sir, of purgatory as believed by the Roman Catholicks?'

Johnson was not a Catholic so his answer is perhaps a little surprising.

'Why, Sir, it is a very harmless doctrine. They are of the opinion that the generality of mankind are neither so obstinately wicked as to deserve everlasting punishment,nor so good as to merit being admitted into the society of blessed spirits; and therefore that God is graciously pleased to allow a middle state, where they may be purified by various degrees of suffering. You see, Sir, there is nothing unreasonable in this.'

To any believer in justification by faith, as examined earlier, that is heresy but the concept of purgatory cannot be overlooked in any serious analysis of penance.

Those in purgatory have repented of their sins but have not yet fully expiated them and so are not yet fit for heaven but to be in purgatory at all is a guaranteed entry to heaven. St Augustine writes 'temporary punishments are suffered by some in this life only, by others after death, by others both now and then.'

Certainly the catacombs provide evidence that the early Christians prayed for the dead which suggests that the idea that penance could be performed after death was one held from the earliest years of the Church. Of course it would not be a voluntary penance!

The principal relevance of purgatory to penance is that it clearly involves expiation through suffering rather than any other means. It is of course too late to expiate sin through reparation at that stage so the soul is purified by fire and torment, leavened only by the certainty of Heaven at the end of it. However there is no teaching that the fire is a literal one. As Leo Trese writes in *The Faith Explained* it is separation from God, even if only for an instant, which is the soul's punishment.

The concept of penance after life on this earth is over is found also in Judaism where there is a belief that the soul has a period of reflection and penance after death. In a rather different form it is found also in Hinduism, where the soul is reincarnated time after time until finally fit for the presence of God. Buddhism has a similar teaching.

The common thread to all these beliefs is the recognition that the soul can leave the body in an unclean state but that only a clean soul can enter the presence of God, therefore there must be some means of expiation after life in the body has ceased.

Expiation through suffering, whether in the hereafter or by being obliged to try again on earth, is also a common theme. By contrast Islam suggests the consequences of the way we have lived will be Heaven or Hell. It further teaches suffering in the grave before judgement but only as a foretaste of the damnation to come not as a means of averting it.

The crucial aspect of the doctrine of purgatory is that one does not enter it unforgiven. One has been fully forgiven through Calvary and belief but it is still necessary to be purified before, forgiven *and* cleansed, one enters God's presence. In a way this is the spiritual equivalent of my observation in Chapter 4 that retribution and forgiveness are not mutually exclusive. As any parent can confirm it is possible to forgive and to punish simultaneously.

Yet the parallel is not an exact one because crucially we are here not talking about punishment but about purification, about a state of cleanliness, about fitness to be with God. The expiation in the afterlife is not about making reparation to God as we would to man but about eliminating the very last traces of all that stands in our way to His presence.

And then comes Heaven which is what it is all about, in its various forms, in most religions. It is about securing a happy and eternal life. It is about not merely believing but actively recognising that this life is but a short precursor to a non-ending one but that the latter can take two forms, Heaven or Hell, and that eventually we must end up in one or the other. Put like that, those who believe that all the answers are in this life are gambling 90-odd years against an eternity. Ladbrokes would never even open such a book.

In a society which no longer has much biblical literacy the concept of Heaven is a vague one: some sort of place where relatives in white night-gowns are waiting bathed in bright light, if we are to take the word of those who have had 'out of body' experiences. The concept of what we have to do to get there is even vaguer. We must just be good, as if any human being can be good in its purest sense, or we must try to be good but somehow without turning to Infinite Goodness as the guide.

Hell? What a barbaric concept! Christ was such a gentle person, forgiving here, healing there, turning the other cheek. Surely He wouldn't let anyone go to such a place? Inconveniently however much of His teaching was about the imperative to avoid exactly that fate, which He had no doubt awaited the unrepentant.

The Devil? A figment of some warped imagination. No such thing really, is there? He belongs to the world of bad fairy tales or old-fashioned morality yarns, doesn't he? But if God is the source of all things good what is the source of all things bad?

So Heaven awaits the pilgrim and the penitent. It is for the imperfect who would be perfect and its big attraction is that in Heaven there is no sadness, no suffering, no guilt and, hallelujah, hallelujah, no penance.